The Story of the Borough

By Leonard Reilly

London Borough of Southwark 2009
Neighbourhood History No.7

ISBN 978-0-905849-44-7
2009

Front cover: St Saviour's church (Southwark Cathedral), 1840.
From the entrance to London Bridge Station.

Inside front cover: Borough High Street, watercolour by William Knox, 1826.

Inside back cover: London Bridge and Borough High Street, 1830.
A view looking south from the bridge while under construction. The view fully shows the extent of the demolitions required to realign the new approach to the bridge. The line of the old approach can be seen clearly on the left-hand side of the image. If this level of redevelopment was not enough, building work to St Saviour's church is also taking place.

Most of the images come from the rich collection held by the Southwark Local History Library. Some have been reproduced before, but many have not. The library gives grateful thanks to those bodies who have allowed their illustrations to be reproduced here. The source of these illustrations is given in their captions. Strenuous efforts have been made to contact the holders of reproduction rights over the images used here. If any rights have been inadvertently infringed, the library offers its apologies.

Contents

Introduction and acknowledgements   1

Early history   4
   Roman Southwark   4
   Saxon and early-medieval Southwark   13
   Medieval Southwark   15

The early-modern period   32
   Townscape   32
   People and society   43
   Economy, industry, commerce and trade   50

The long nineteenth century: 1800-1939   55
   People and society   55
   Local government   73
   Churches and religious life
   Public buildings: hospitals and prisons   81
   Daily life   85
   Economy, employment and industry   87
   Transport   96

Recent generations   107
   World War II   107
   People and housing   109
   A community and its services   111
   Industry, business and commerce   115
   Government, justice and hospitals   125
   Transport   128

Looking forward and back   130

Sources   132
Index   134

Key to map

1   Southwark Cathedral
2   Site of St Olave's church
3   Hay's Wharf and Galleria
4   More London
5   Former St Thomas' Hospital, church and Old Operating Theatre
6   King's Head Yard
7   White Hart Yard
8   George Inn
9   Site of Tabard Inn
10   War Memorial, site of St Margaret's church
11   Calvert's Buildings
12   Hop Exchange
13   Octavia Hill Cottages
14/15 St Saviour's and St Joseph's schools
16   King's Arms public house
17   Site of the last Marshalsea Prison
       now John Harvard and Local History Libraries
18   St Hugh's Church, Charterhouse in Southwark
19   Mint Street Adventure Playground, site of workhouse
20   Brandon House, site of Suffolk Place
21   St George's church
22   Charles Dickens School
23   Scovell Estate, site of King's Bench Prison
24   Police station, site of 'Stone's End'
25   Henry Wood Hall, former Holy Trinity church
26   Site of Horsemonger Lane Gaol
27   St Saviour's and St Olave's school

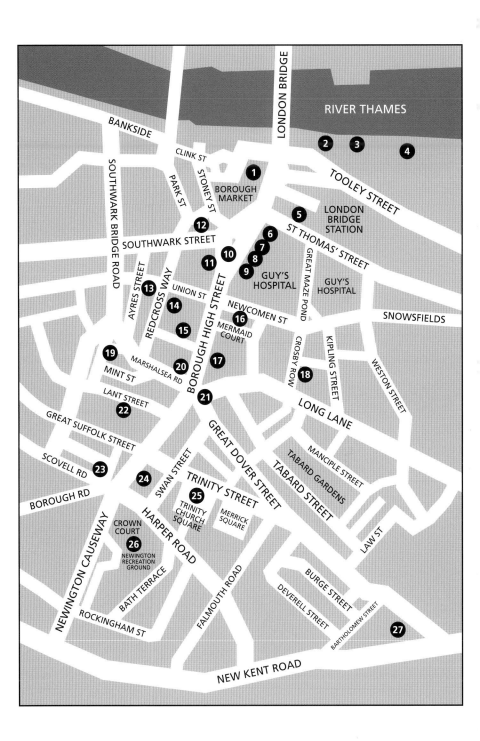

London Borough of Southwark Neighbourhood Histories

1   The Story of Camberwell
2   The Story of Dulwich
3   The Story of Peckham and Nunhead
4   The Story of Walworth
5   The Story of Bermondsey
6   The Story of Rotherhithe
7   The Story of the Borough
8   The Story of Bankside

Introduction

While it is widely acknowledged that the Borough is one of the most historic areas in London, there is little agreement as to where exactly it is. In the popular mind it is lumped together with London Bridge or with Bankside, part of the London Borough of Southwark across the River Thames from the City of London. But it is hard to be more precise than that. Unfortunately, the study of modern or historic administrative or parochial boundaries and structures is of little help. Until 1965 the area discussed here was split between two Metropolitan Boroughs; before 1900 it was split between at least four parishes, and in the medieval period it was administered by a number of independent manors. Nor are we helped by the name the Borough. In the medieval period a borough was a self-governing town, with its own council, the right to elect MPs and usually a charter from the Crown confirming these rights. However, Southwark's administration was far from unified and it never had a charter, although it could elect two MPs.

A useful start for our definition is provided by the boundaries of the ancient parliamentary constituency, which included three of the town's five manors: the King's manor, the Great Liberty manor and the Guildable manor. The other two manors, the Clink and Paris Garden, were outside the area. However, the Borough is more than an administrative unit, it is a popular and cultural one. It is a mixture of the formal and popular boundaries that this book follows.

This book defines the Borough as the area of the ancient constituency of Southwark along with the northern part of its neighbour St Mary, Newington, that was on, or near the town's main road, Borough High Street. Strictly, the high street extended south for about a mile from London Bridge to so-called Stone's End approximately on the site of the police station at the high street's southern end. However, we go slightly farther south to the court buildings on Newington Causeway because of their direct descent from the Surrey County prison. We also go south-east down Great Dover Street, strictly part of the Borough and because its institutions, businesses and social history share the experience with the area just to the west.

Having established 'the where', what of 'the what'? In character the Borough was close, noisy, crowded, unhealthy, vigorous, independent, and above all a relentless vortex of activity and movement of people and animals, goods and vehicles, factories and traders. It was an intensely urban area; in part a suburb of London and in part a self-contained community with its own government, economy, society and character.

This book is part of a long-running series, started by Southwark's first Local Studies Librarian, Mary Boast. There are companion volumes to the west and the east: *The Story of Bankside* and *The Story of Bermondsey* respectively. This book aims to dovetail with them. However, they in turn do not rigorously follow formal boundaries. (Bankside stretches as far inland as St George's Circus and Bermondsey discusses the riverside wharves as far west as London Bridge.)

This book therefore excludes the Bankside area to the west and it shades off into Tooley Street in the east. Inevitably there is some overlap and even duplication with other areas (the Cathedral is featured here and in Bankside; the wharves and warehouses of the Upper Pool feature here and in Bermondsey) and because it is necessary to discuss the wider London and national context of events, to make sense of the local ones.

In addition to the Neighbourhood History series, the Southwark area has a solid presence in historical literature. It was mentioned by London's first significant historian, John Stow, in the late 16th century, in great detail by William Rendle in the 19th century. It is covered by two volumes of the Survey of London and academically the medieval and early-modern periods are discussed by Martha Carlin and Jeremy Boulton respectively. It also features strongly in more recently written histories of London. However, it lacks an up-to-date discussion of its main themes for the adult reader. This book aims to do that, and so supplement and complement but not to supersede the more journalistic coverage in the numerous tourist guides to the area.

Despite the claim of being one of the most historic areas in London, there is little obvious evidence of this distinguished antiquity. However, even a casual observer is likely to assemble a number of observations and questions. They would notice the name 'high street' and its unusual length but observe that it is (perhaps refreshingly) clear of the usual occupants of the standard British high street. They would notice that it leads to what is generally known to be London's oldest bridge. They might observe that the junction near its southern end is where the A2 and the A3 roads meet. They might notice the unusual number of narrow and long alleys running at right angles off the high street, like ribs from a backbone. They should notice that there are two very distinguished churches within 1200 m of each other at either end of the high street. They would notice that one of these churches is of great antiquity (and is a cathedral) and that there are two seemingly medieval buildings in the alleys on the west side of the high street. (However, the immediate conclusions one might draw from these features are unlikely to be wholly accurate!) They might even notice a number of plaques pointing out features of historic interest.

What will be apparent is a very wide mix of building styles, periods and functions. And what follows from these and the genuine antiquity is the clear conclusion that the area has undergone constant redevelopment and change during its 2,000 year history and it is this constant flux that makes the district such a fascinating and challenging one to study.

In fact, Borough High Street is London's oldest high street and has experienced a more interesting, colourful and varied history than all its namesakes. This has involved Roman occupation, medieval prelates, the comings and goings of countless travellers, rebellions, fires, royal processions, prisons and their inmates, trade, industry, poverty and a continual churn of redevelopment.

The questions asked and hopefully answered are ones that have come to me as an observer and reader, but more pertinently have been posed directly or indirectly to myself and colleagues by the thousands of visitors and enquirers to the Southwark Local History Library, where I had the privilege to work for seven years as its Local Studies Librarian. Without the stimulation posed by these enquiries this book would be poorer, but possibly shorter.

The book tackles its material chronologically in four long chapters and then divides each thematically to deal with the recurring main themes of townscape, population, economy and society. Where possible it makes reference to modern street names and so a street map (but ideally a street map and a pair of walking shoes) would make a useful complement.

In addition to my thanks to the library's now anonymous readers, I must thank the staff there: Stephen Humphrey, Ruth Jenkins, Stephen Potter and Bob Askew, for their help in researching this and for their encouraging and critical comments on the draft text. Stephen Humphrey also took on the role of meticulous copy-editor in the latter stages of this book's production. The book was designed by Carol Enright, whose visual flair, calmness under pressure and respect for deadlines make her a joy to work with. I alone take responsibility for the errors of fact, interpretation and omission.

CHAPTER 1

Early history

ROMAN SOUTHWARK

The Romans founded the first urban settlement at Southwark. This was the earliest, the largest and the most enduring Roman riverside settlement on the southern shore of the Thames. It managed to be all these things despite the unpromising geography of the area the Romans chose to develop, which was low lying, marshy and dominated by the River Thames. The river was tidal to London, but probably no farther upstream and, on the south bank, there was no clear distinction between river and dry land for maybe half a mile inland of the low water mark. The edge of the permanent dry land was approximately at the line of the modern Tabard Street and Marshalsea Road. Instead, the river flowed through a series of braided channels and around and, at high tide, partly over, a complex of sand and gravel islands. There were two main islands in a roughly north–south alignment with the dividing channel between them approximately on the line of the modern Southwark Street.

The landscape the Romans occupied had developed over many centuries. It is impossible to be precise about exact features and dates, but it seems that the sand and gravel islands took shape at about 9,000 BC at a time when the river's tidal limit was considerably downstream of modern London. It is likely that the edge of uninterrupted and permanent dry land was the same as in the Roman period and that this area was wooded. While the Romans were the first to establish an urban culture in the area, they were not the first settlers. There is evidence of ancient agricultural activities on the south side of the river at Bermondsey and at Hopton Street in Southwark, but the evidence is uncertain, being scattered over time and place.

The Romans invaded Britain in AD 43 and approached the Thames from the south, most probably along Watling Street, which they built as they went. In its approach to the Thames, Watling Street followed the edge of the permanently dry ground. Some historians have thought that the first Thames crossing – a ferry – was downstream of Southwark at modern Lambeth. However, what became Londinium, opposite Southwark on the site of the modern City of London, offered the area's best natural advantages for a permanent, large-scale settlement. It had hilly, dry land suitable for buildings and a deep tidal river that allowed easy access and mooring for sea-going ships. The presence of Southwark's sand and gravel islands must have influenced this choice of a site as they enabled the building of a road to a point where the river (at c. 360 m wide) was narrow enough to be bridged. A bridge was essential to the Romans as a ferry had neither the capacity nor security to supply Londinium and beyond – all the province's main roads to the north west and east radiated from Londinium. The province needed troops, (who landed on and marched to Londinium from the south coast along Watling and Stane Streets), stone building materials (ragstone and sandstone from the Kent and Sussex Weald), iron (also smelted in the Weald) and grain.

An artist's impression of Roman Southwark, c. AD 120, by Peter Froste.
Roman London, after redevelopment and showing all the major buildings.
This is a view from the South East.
Illustration: Museum of London/Peter Froste.

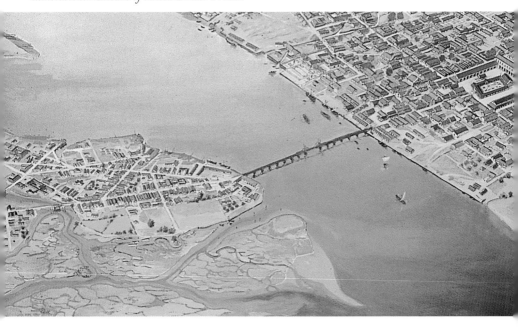

The first London bridge was built very soon after the invasion. The development of a bridgehead settlement at Southwark soon followed. The earliest buildings were of low status and flimsy materials but after AD 60 the settlement expanded with the construction of more substantial, higher status buildings. The settlement contracted in the years leading up to AD 410, the date at which Rome ceased to offer military support to its British province, and the settlement was abandoned.

Our knowledge of Roman Southwark has increased greatly in recent years. The information we have is still being added to and so the conclusions we can draw from it are constantly being revised. Even the precise shape and character of the natural geography was not fully understood until the 1980s. This has been due to a significant increase in archaeology, stimulated by the huge amount of redevelopment taking place in the area. Each new building scheme requires an archaeological investigation and the additional information provided has revised our conclusions about the settlement. The archaeology that took place in the late 1990s during the building of the new ticket hall for London Bridge Station for the Jubilee Line extension provided the single biggest amount of new data. (The Jubilee Line has also been a major stimulus to new building, so generating further archaeological opportunities.) It is now agreed that Roman Southwark was larger and of greater importance than had been previously thought. Despite this, only 5% of the settlement's area has been excavated and there are no conclusive answers to many fundamental questions such as the settlement's economic and administrative status, its relationship to Londinium, the size of its population, the pattern of its expansion and contraction over time, the extent of its public buildings or its facilities for trade, commerce, industry or worship. There is uncertainty about the line, status and destination of the roads. It is not even known if the Romans gave the Southwark area a name to distinguish it from Londinium.

Roads and bridges

The Roman bridge's southern footings have not been found, but the positions of the road approaches on either side of the river and of finds of Roman coins on the river bed suggest that the bridge was about 75 m downstream of its modern counterpart. It is thought there was a sequence of three bridge structures: a timber bridge, which continued until c. AD 50; then a temporary bridge, probably of light decking on a floating pontoon, and finally, from c. AD 120, a more substantial structure supported by stone or brick piers about 12 m apart and with a drawbridge to allow the passage of larger ships. Each bridge had wooden decking which would have needed periodic maintenance and replacement. The bridge's decline is unclear, but evidence from coins found on the river bed suggests it may have fallen into disuse before the Romans abandoned Londinium in AD 410. As well as facilitating communication, the bridge was also a major defensive feature, effectively blocking the Thames against any water-borne forces.

The bridge was approached from the south by two roads. The more important, indeed the backbone of the whole settlement, from then to the present, followed the highest dry land, approximately on the line of modern Borough High Street. The road had foundations of oak and alder and a gravel surface; small bridges crossed the channels between the islands. Roughly where the permanent dry land started and somewhere close to St George the Martyr church, there was a road junction, although its precise location is still to be found. At the junction the road forked: Stane Street went south towards Chichester via the Elephant and Castle and Kennington, and Watling Street went south east, following the line of the modern Tabard Street and the Old Kent Road, crossing Deptford Creek five miles away and on to Dover. The line of Stane Street south of St George's church is uncertain as no positive trace of the Roman road has been found between there and the Elephant and Castle.

The second approach went south-west from the bridgehead, but there is only evidence for it going as far as the modern cathedral. A small part of it is exposed outside the cathedral's north-eastern corner in a permanent display of archaeological features uncovered during the building of the cathedral's new chapter house. It has been surmised that the second approach road either went to another river crossing at Lambeth, or linked with Stane Street, or possibly just ended at a wharf at the edge of the island – we do not know.

Whatever the detail of the roads' precise courses, they followed the most direct route allowed by the natural geography between the bridged crossing of the Thames and the coast. That the Romans undertook such major engineering feats so early in Londinium's development shows how essential land communication from the south was to the viability of their new settlement.

Expansion and consolidation

In its early decades Roman Southwark's buildings were of low status, made from timber and clay, and roofed with thatch or tile. At this time, development seems to have been confined to the sides of the main road and to the north island. A large find of Roman coins from the 1st century suggests a military presence or function – hardly surprising considering the importance of the bridge and its approaches. Further evidence for a military presence is a stone inscribed with the names of members of a military guild. It was found at the site of Winchester Palace and dates from the 3rd century. However, there is no evidence for planned earth or walled defences, or for a fort or permanent garrison. This contrasts strongly with the walled and stoutly-defended city of Londinium and perhaps suggests that the Romans calculated any attacks would come from the north. It may have been that they also decided that Southwark's marshy landscape offered too difficult a terrain over which an aggressor would mount an attack, or that they built no defences because they were prepared to sacrifice Southwark to aggressors and only defend London north of the river. We just do not know.

Two events in the later-1st century significantly enhanced Southwark's fortunes. The first paradoxically was a major fire that destroyed very many of the settlement's buildings. This is most likely to have been the work of the native Briton Queen Boudica and her followers, during her violent and bloody rebellion against Roman rule in AD 60. Tacitus's account of this states that it was decided by the military authorities that, because the Roman forces were inferior to the rebels, the Romans would *"sacrifice the single city of Londinium to save the province as a whole"*. The second was the slightly later decision to make Londinium the capital of Roman Britain.

These events stimulated a phase of rebuilding with higher status buildings, often in stone. Their features included mosaic floors, decorated wall plaster, under floor heating and baths. In London Bridge Station concourse in Joiner Street there is a display of some of the most interesting finds made during the building of the Jubilee Line extension. It has been suggested that the large complex of buildings at 15-23 Southwark Street (on the south side of the north island and conveniently between the two major roads from the bridge), which included a large courtyard, could have been a major public building. This building has been dated to AD 72-4. There is also evidence of land reclamation taking place in the later 1st century on the east side of the north island, suggesting that most suitable land was in use by then.

Above: The Londoners' stone.

Right: The tin of Roman face cream found during excavations at Tabard Square. Illustrations: ©Pre-Construct Archaeology.

At its fullest extent Roman Southwark is thought to have been 30 acres (12 hectares) and so about 10% of the size of Roman London. However even that must be imprecise as the settlement had no administrative or physical boundary.

There is considerable evidence for a range of industrial activity in Roman Southwark, although its scale suggests it was fulfilling a purely local need. There was metal-working in both iron and copper near Park Street in the 2nd century and, in the 4th century, a smithy alongside Borough High Street. These produced both tools and decorative objects. There was a pottery kiln at Borough High Street. Curiously there is no evidence of agriculture in the near vicinity. Excavations have revealed many pits and small quarries where gravel was extracted for building and to resurface the road.

The presence of the Thames meant the settlement would inevitably have a major trading function. There are many examples of timber waterfronts, substantial quantities of jars containing goods from all over the Roman Empire, including olives, wine and fish. One jar found near Winchester Palace retained its contents of Spanish mackerel, imported from the Mediterranean. There was a large wooden warehouse found near Park Street. Its floor was partly below the Roman ground level making it suitable for keeping and preserving perishable goods. Along Borough High Street there was a 40 m long building with stone colonnades, possibly used as a market. Wheat and animal bones found at the station ticket hall site suggest the presence of a baker's and a butcher's.

Further new evidence of Southwark's previously under-estimated importance to the Romans was the discovery of a major temple complex dating from the mid 2nd century at the junction of Tabard Street and Long Lane. Previously the only conclusive evidence of religious worship were finds of religious sculptures, notably of Neptune or Oceanus from the crypt of the cathedral, raising the intriguing possibility that the site was used for worship in pre-Christian times.

Among the finds at the temple was the unexpected, highly unusual and intriguing one of a small tin pot part-filled with cream. It is unclear if the cream was used in religious worship or was simply for cosmetic vanity; what is clear is that it was recently used as there is still a groove across its surface where a Roman finger scooped up a dollop before applying it. The tin container makes the item particularly interesting, because tin corrodes easily and because it was a precious metal, showing that this was an item belonging to somebody of considerable wealth.

Roman burial sites give clues as to population size and possibly the status and beliefs of those buried or cremated, although these subjects are very difficult to interpret. Their location can also assist with plotting the extent of the settlement as Roman burial grounds were very often on the periphery of the built-up area and very frequently along or near main roads. There is a ring of burials stretching in an arc from Tabard Street in the east and Swan Street to Lant Street in the south (all on the 'mainland') showing the fullest size of the area settled by the Romans. Later burials found at the junction of Redcross Way and Southwark Street (on the north island) show the contraction of the later period. The most impressive cemetery was on a site between Great Dover Street and Tabard Street and, being close to Watling Street, is consistent with proximity to main roads. As well as 26 bodies and 8 cremations, there were two large mausolea, one capped with an acorn-shaped stone feature. The largest cemetery was at America Street (south of Southwark Street and west of Southwark Bridge Road). It contained 170 burials from the 2nd and 3rd centuries. The cemetery found at Lant Street contained 88 burials and two cremations and dates from the 2nd to the 4th centuries.

The ever-present river meant considerable effort went into keeping dry areas dry and maximising the watercourses for transport. There are many surviving waterside timber barriers, called revetments, built to prevent erosion and inundation; examples were at the south-west side of the north island, the north side of the south island and the east side of the north island at Guy's Channel, where a man-made waterfront over 30 m long was found. Boats were used for transport and a large, flat-bottomed lighter was found in the so-called Guy's Channel in 1958. Wooden bridges spanned the watercourses and connected the islands.

There is no positive evidence either way to say whether Southwark was independent of or integral to the Londinium administration. The absence of any obvious administrative buildings, the fact that Tacitus does not distinguish between Londinium and Southwark and the fact that the so-called Londoners' stone was excavated in Southwark at the junction of Long Lane and Tabard Street, all suggest that Southwark was seen as part of Londinium. The place where the Londoners' stone was found is marked by a plaque in the ground in the Berkeley Homes' development.

Southwark (and Londinium) contracted in the 3rd and 4th century; it has been estimated that the population halved. In AD 410 Rome withdrew military and administrative support to the province. An appropriate feature for this period of decline and of the abandonment that followed

An artist's reconstruction of the mausoleum between Great Dover Street and Tabard Street.
Illustration: Museum of London Archaeology.

is one of the area's last and most perplexing archaeological features: a layer, up to a metre thick, of dark loam soil of unknown origin and purpose. Southwark and indeed Londinium were abandoned after the Empire withdrew military support. The bridge fell, or maybe had already fallen into disrepair, and the buildings, roads and water defences all decayed. What had been a thriving commercial, manufacturing, residential, probably military and possibly administrative centre for four centuries gave way to the forces of nature.

Southwark made a major contribution to Londinium. It clearly provided secure access to the bridge and the number and occasional size and quality of later, high-status buildings suggest that the population included the wealthy or powerful. While there is some evidence for industrial, administrative and military activity, Southwark does not seem to have been overwhelmingly characterised by any of them. One might expect features associated with travel, such as inns or customs posts, but if present, they await discovery. The presence of warehouses and the obvious easy access to the river suggest the potential for trade and commerce. We can be sure that Roman Southwark's fortunes rose and fell with those of Londinium, and it is possible this was the only period until modern times that Southwark was an integral part of London, a situation that later rulers of the City of London might have looked at with envy.

SAXON AND EARLY MEDIEVAL SOUTHWARK

Archaeological and written sources are silent on Southwark for more than two centuries after the Romans' abandonment in 410. The area was uninhabited for all this time and buildings, roads and river defences were abandoned and decayed. The walled City of London was similarly abandoned. Repopulation started in the 7th century, but to the west of London around the Aldwych. At this time, southern England was controlled by a number of Saxon kingdoms, some Christian, some not, who were frequently in conflict with one another.

The main catalyst for the re-occupation of London and for the re-establishment of Southwark was the Saxon response to the Viking raids. These raids started in the 9th century and continued irregularly for the next three hundred years. The Vikings have a place in popular history as savage aggressors and their raids were undoubtedly destructive, brutal and bloody and their rule as colonisers exploitative in the extreme. However the Vikings were also sophisticated traders and built up a network of water borne commerce over northern Europe, eastern Russia and into the Mediterranean. After the 840s London was subject to regular raids and the city was captured and occupied by them from 877. London was recaptured by King Alfred of Wessex in 886. Immediately after this date, or some time before 914 (historians are divided on this matter) a major defensive earthwork was constructed in Southwark. This was part of a series of defences across the kingdom of Wessex and they are referred to in a document of 914 called the Burghal Hidage. This is the first mention by name of Southwark: Suthringa geweorche: the [defensive] work of the people of Surrey. Accepting the Burghal Hidage's measurements (and there is dispute as to how to interpret them), the fortifications were nearly a mile and a half long – roughly enough to enclose the two Roman islands, though ditches found by archaeologists suggest the area to be much smaller. Sadly no garrison or defensive buildings have been found, but it is probable that the site would have been actively manned by troops.

The precise date of the Burghal Hidage is perhaps less significant than the implication that a bridge was in place before the construction of the earthwork. The bridge's presence generated the need to defend its southern approach for travellers and to prevent any attackers from by-passing it overland to the south. It is known that the bridge was rebuilt by c. 1000 as the timbers used have been dated to 987-1032. It is possible that the Roman brick foundations remained and if they did the reconstruction of some kind of structure might not have been a hugely difficult task. The bridge demonstrated its effectiveness as a defensive structure twice in the early 11th century. In 1014 attackers attempted to pull it down by attaching grappling irons to it and rowing away – the source of the nursery rhyme, *London Bridge is falling down*. Two years later, when another group of attackers were unable to capture the bridge they dragged their boats overland across Southwark, perhaps making use of any surviving water channels around the islands. Despite its importance for defence and communication, the Saxon and early medieval bridge and its bridgehead were flimsy structures, vulnerable to erosion and requiring constant maintenance.

The Burghal Hidage also bequeathed the area a second name: the Borough. The origin of the word burgh means a place of shelter or defence, exactly the circumstances that apply to Southwark. A Borough is also an administrative unit. Historians are divided as to what qualified a town for borough status. In the early-medieval period, a minster, a mint and a market were crucial and Southwark had all of these. Later, however, a borough came to mean a unified self-governing town, with a royal charter confirming this status, which could send MPs to parliament. Despite the continuous and widespread use of the name 'the Borough of Southwark' and its right from 1295 to elect its own MPs, Southwark was far from a unified or self-governing body (in fact it was quite the opposite). It never had a royal charter and so, ironically, was never a borough in the later sense.

An important feature of this time was the River Thames's role as a boundary between the Saxon kingdoms of Mercia to the north and Wessex to the south. Hereafter, Southwark was administratively separate from London. It was in the Diocese of Winchester, not London, the kingdom of Wessex, not Mercia and, when counties emerged, in the County of Surrey. This separate and increasingly independent identity was to frustrate the City of London for centuries to come.

By the end of the 10th century the foundations of medieval Southwark were laid as two essential elements for the town's success were in place: defence, provided by the earthworks, and a commercial role serving travellers using the bridge.

MEDIEVAL SOUTHWARK

During the medieval period, roughly the late 10th century to the mid 16th century, Southwark evolved into a major town independent of London, with its own distinctive economic and commercial functions, a complex administrative structure of five independent manors and of five equally independent parishes, an ethnically mixed population and a reputation for crime and lawlessness.

Topography and townscape

Southwark's Saxon and early medieval administrators faced at least one challenge in common with their Roman predecessors: how to defend the settlement against the river. Towards the end of the Roman period, it is thought that the river level fell, but periodic floods took place – in 1014 there was a major flood and in 1097 the bridge was swept away. These circumstances undermined Southwark's potential as a viable settlement and the only solution was a secure river wall and good drainage of the low-lying land. This was achieved through a system of drainage ditches, which also served as boundaries and the construction of a river wall, the line of which was not stabilised until the 13th century.

As in the Roman period the higher dry ground influenced the layout of the town. The main artery was the high street, called Long Southwark until the 16th century. Tooley Street, perhaps a corruption of an earlier name 'St Olave's Street' (itself a dedication of one of the parish churches), ran east from the bridgehead and Bankside ran west from the bridgehead and followed the river wall. At the south end of the high street the road divided. One road went south to Newington – from the 13th century this was known as Blackman Street and terminated at Stone's End, possibly the end of the maintained gravelled surface, thereafter continuing as a track across open land towards Walworth. The other road ran south-east along Kent (later Tabard) Street. Long Lane, previously White Street, evolved in later centuries.

One important characteristic of medieval Southwark was the large number of temporary residents, visitors and travellers, and the buildings that were there to serve them. These visitors and travellers came from all parts of society: the most distinguished were important churchmen and other magnates, who had their town houses here, down to temporary visitors or travellers approaching or leaving London, who stayed in one of the many inns along the high street.

Southwark's most senior temporarily resident cleric was the Bishop of Winchester and appropriately he had the most impressive property in the whole town. His presence and property, Winchester Palace, just west of the cathedral, are described more fully in the companion to this volume, *The Story of Bankside*. In addition there was a cluster of important houses on Tooley Street occupied by other senior clerics including the Prior of Lewes, the Abbot of Battle Abbey, the Prior of Christ Church, Canterbury and the Abbot of St Augustine's, Canterbury. Situated off the high street were the properties occupied by the Abbot of Beaulieu and the Archdeacon of Surrey. Important secular residents included the Warenne family, Earls of Surrey and, for a time, King Edward II, who lived at a house at Horselydown at the east end of Tooley Street. Many of these houses were called inns, and some later assumed the function we understand by this term. Generally they were substantial multi-building developments, often set back from the main road and fronted by shops.

After the Bishop of Winchester's Palace, the two most substantial houses were away from the town centre. In the mid-15th century Sir John Fastolf built a moated mansion house on the site of Edward II's palace at the east end of St Olave's parish in Horselydown. This later came into the possession of the Bishop of Winchester. An equally grand and equally short-lived mansion was that of the Brandon family, later holders of the title of Duke of Suffolk. In the early 16th century, Thomas Brandon and his successor and nephew Charles built a large house opposite St George's church at the southern end of the high street and created a large hunting park. They left in 1536 and the property changed hands frequently thereafter and was broken up 20 years later.

Priory, hospital and parishes

The emergence of Southwark's ecclesiastical institutions is as hazy as the emergence of its administrative ones. Today Southwark is dominated by one of the finest medieval buildings in south London, Southwark Cathedral. Before 1905 it was the parish church of St Saviour and before that the Priory Church of St Mary Overie. Domesday Book mentions a monasterium or minster (a minster was a community of priests that gave church services over a large geographical area) but it is not clear whether this was the institution on the site of the present cathedral.

What is more certain is that whatever institution existed here was re-founded c.1106 as a priory of Augustinian clergy. There is little evidence of the earliest building as it was destroyed in a fire in 1212.

This was the first of a series of hazards, real and threatened, that make it remarkable that any ecclesiastical institution has survived on the site, let alone such an important one. At its greatest extent the priory church (which had much the same footprint as the modern cathedral) was supplemented to the north by the convent buildings, which provided accommodation for the clergy. These were accessed by gates opening to the east and to the west. To the south was a parish church dedicated to St Mary Magdalene, which served laity within the priory precinct.

The priory enjoyed a close and good relationship with the Bishop of Winchester, in whose diocese Southwark lay and who had his London townhouse close by. He also controlled the Clink manor to the west. The bishop was responsible for appointing the prior and used the priory church for important ceremonies. The priory also enjoyed good relations with the town, providing it with a chapel, a burial ground and a school. The priory was closed down in 1539 during the religious upheavals known as the Reformation and instigated by Henry VIII. The priory's closure was remarkable for at least two events. First was the huge pension of £100 a year awarded to the last prior, an extraordinary payment that Henry VIII must have hoped would ensure a trouble-free dissolution and succeeding years. Second was the survival of the actual building – albeit with a different function – unusual at the time, when monastic houses were as valuable for their stone (for reuse in building projects) as for their lands.

The priory was also responsible for the foundation of one of the most important and long-lived charitable institutions in south London: St Thomas' Hospital. St Thomas', (now in Lambeth) and its daughter institution, Guy's Hospital continue to this day to provide care to tens of thousands of local residents.

St Thomas' Hospital was founded in the priory precinct in the 1170s, with the aim of providing care for the sick and poor in body and soul. It was dedicated to the martyr St Thomas of Canterbury. After the fire of 1212, it was moved and refounded as an independent body on the east side of the high street. It was about nine acres in size and occupied a site on the north of the modern St Thomas' Street. It also had its own burial ground. Like the priory, the clergy were Augustinians and, like the priory, it came under the patronage of the Bishop of Winchester. The hospital was consistently poor and suffered from maladministration and scandals, most notably in the early-16th century under the master Richard Mabott. The hospital had its own church with the same dedication to St Thomas, and the church doubled in function as a ward. In the middle ages it became a parish in its own right. As a religious house it was closed down at the dissolution of the monasteries but the hospital was revived in 1551 under the control of the City of London and was rededicated to St Thomas the Apostle.

The priory and the hospital both had parish churches attached to them to provide services to those living in their respective confines. Southwark also had three other parishes, which were much larger. The three churches were all on or near the high street, while the parishes extended to either side. All three are first heard of at roughly the same time in the late 11th and early 12th centuries.

Borough High Street, c. 1550 by Anthonis van den Wyngaerde.
This view is both highly detailed and hugely distorted. Unduly prominent is Suffolk Place (it's the building with round towers, centre left), while the high street has been hugely foreshortened.
Illustration: Ashmolean Museum, University of Oxford.

THE STORY OF THE BOROUGH

To the north-east was St Olave's parish and the church stood on the riverfront east of the bridge. The dedication is to the Norse Olave, one of a number of dedications in London that might result from Olaf's defence of London against King Cnut of Denmark in 1014.

St Margaret's parish church was in the middle of the high street where the high street forks, just south of the junction with modern Southwark Street. The parish included virtually all of the riverfront west of the bridge i.e. all of the manors of Paris Garden and the Clink. By the early-16th century the church building had become dilapidated and the parishioners, along with the much smaller number from St Mary Magdalene, joined together to purchase the priory church of St Mary Overie to make it their new parish church dedicated to St Saviour. Southwark therefore had one of the biggest parish churches in England, but neither St Olave's nor St George's parish was willing to surrender to its bigger neighbour, despite the fact that St Saviour could easily accommodate their combined congregations, that their churches were in need of repair and that the expense of St Saviour's upkeep was way beyond the means of its parishioners.

St George's was the largest but least built-up parish. Alone of all the medieval parish churches it is the only one where a church still stands on its original site today. The site is certainly an impressive one, largely thanks to modern road planners who have left it in glorious isolation at the junction of Borough High Street with Long Lane and Tabard Street. The bulk of the parish comprised the marshy St George's Fields to the west but it also included a long strip following Kent Street and the Old Kent Road to the south east. The church is first heard of in 1122.

Each parish managed its own affairs. Responsibility for church fabric lay with the churchwardens, other parochial functions lay with vestrymen and care of the poor with the overseers. From the 16th century onwards the parish became the dominant unit of local administration.

One problem faced by all the parishes was that of maintaining a suitable burial ground. Burial grounds were usually adjacent to the church, but as the town urbanised and the population grew, the churchyards became full and the parishes were forced to purchase additional plots of land. St Margaret's bought an acre of land in 1533 and St Olave's parish bought additional plots in 1520 and 1538.

Commercial Inns

While Tooley Street was a centre for the larger private houses, the high street was the location for commercial inns used by travellers or visitors, sometimes temporary and sometimes staying for extended periods. It was no surprise that inn keeping developed as a major enterprise in Southwark. Travellers were unable to access or leave London during the hours of darkness and when the drawbridge on London Bridge was closed; within the City its authorities imposed strict regulation on those running inns, and in addition Southwark had more land available to keep and feed horses. Demand for temporary accommodation also grew as a result of London's developing status as the national centre for government, trade, business and the law.

There is strong evidence of inn keeping in Southwark from the early 14th century, although it is most likely visitors were put up in what were effectively inns before this date. It has been calculated that there were more than two dozen inns or drinking houses on the high street by the end of the 14th century. This number had expanded by 1600 and in the 17th century Thomas Dekker described Borough High Street as 'a continuous ale house with not a shop to be seen'.

Four of the inns have become particularly well known. The George because it has survived, the White Hart, from its description in Charles Dickens's *Pickwick Papers*, and appearance in Shakespeare's *Henry VI*, the Queen's Head as the property of John Harvard and the Tabard as the place of departure for Chaucer's pilgrims. The Tabard was one of the large and more luxurious inns and its keeper Harry Bailey was a person in history as a well as fiction as he was MP for Southwark in 1375-6 and again in 1378.

Typically the inn buildings had a narrow frontage to the high street leading to a yard and surrounding buildings at right angles to the main road. Some inns were conversions from private buildings, some purpose-built. Some were sizeable; Chaucer's pilgrims, who were lavishly hosted at the Tabard, numbered 29 people, and it was claimed that some inns could accommodate 100 guests. The larger ones extended for more than 100 m back from their entrances to the road.

Inn keepers offered three services: lodging, food and stabling. Accommodation ranged from the temporary, for arriving or departing travellers, to the semi-permanent, for those with extended business in London. By tradition, and later by regulation, lodging incurred only a minimum charge, but big profits could be made on food, stabling and the hire of horses. Inn keepers competed over the quality, variety and quantity of their food and drink and charged accordingly. There was a constant demand from travellers for fresh horses and the open spaces on the east and west side of the high street were used for stabling and grazing the hundreds of animals that carried and pulled visitors or goods to and from the Borough. The inn keepers' freedom to charge what the market would bear for food for both residents and horses was in contrast to the arrangements in the City, where such matters were strictly controlled.

The emphasis was on providing high-quality accommodation and so poorer travellers, particularly those on foot, often found themselves priced out or made unwelcome. In response to this, from the mid 16th century the authorities required brewhouse keepers to offer accommodation to travellers, so increasing capacity and offering accommodation of a more affordable type.

The northern part of the plan of Long Southwark, c.1542, from William Rendle Old Southwark and its people *based on a view held by the Duchy of Lancaster. The view looks south from the River Thames; note the prominence given to the inns.*

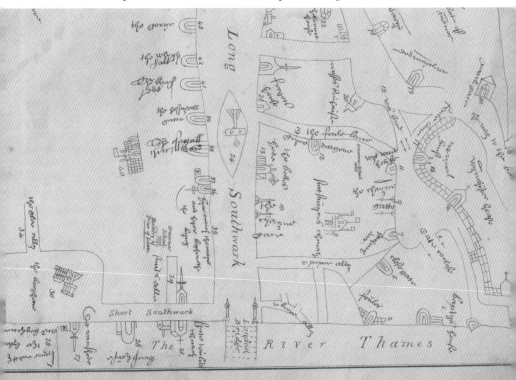

The inns remained an enduring feature of the high street until the mid 19th century when the arrival of the railway made them redundant. Many vestiges are clearly visible even today in the form of narrow alleys, particularly on the east side of the high street, many leading into the grounds of Guy's Hospital. The high street still has its fair share of pub buildings and two, the King's Head and the George, have the orientation of the medieval inns. Neither is original: the King's Head is a Victorian rebuild and The George was rebuilt after one of the devastating fires suffered by the high street in the 17th century. Calvert's Buildings on the west side of the high street includes some remains of the Elizabethan inn called the Goat. However, the authentic medieval-looking half-timbered building at Chapel Court is a convincing pastiche built in the 1980s!

Inn keeping also supported a large range of related activities: brewing, victualling, laundry, cart repair and horse keeping. Brewing was represented through larger commercial brewhouses, which had a wholesale as well as a retail function and smaller alehouses. Victuallers supplied all manner of foodstuffs from fixed premises. Their activities were complemented by the traders in Southwark's street market.

Prisons

The Borough had a second population group living away from their normal place of existence, though this time usually against their will: prisoners. The area has played host to no fewer than six major prisons over the centuries. Probably the best known is the Clink, the private prison of the Bishop of Winchester's manor. It is discussed in the companion volume, *The Story of Bankside*. The Marshalsea Prison and the King's Bench Prison were both royal prisons. The Borough Compter was run by the City of London, and Surrey County ran the Surrey County jail and the Surrey House of Correction.

A number of common threads run through the history of the prisons, and these contexts are significantly different to the function and position of prisons today. The first, as is apparent from the various institutions that ran the prisons, was that there were many different jurisdictions, each with rights of imprisonment – royal, manorial and county jurisdictions are all represented; the second that prisons were not run directly by the jurisdiction, but often as a franchise where the gaoler had the potential to make profit from his enterprise – this temptation was usually ruthlessly exploited to the unlawful disadvantage of the unfortunate inmates.

Related to this was the fact that prisoners were not locked up at the expense of the convicting court, or the prison, but at their own expense and an inability to pay their fees meant longer imprisonment and an obvious and inescapable cycle of entrapment; prisons were usually in private premises adapted for the purpose, not purpose-built; the gaoler in times of spare capacity could take prisoners from other jurisdictions and in this way a number of the prisons evolved into debtors' prisons.

The Marshalsea was the prison of the court of the Knight Marshal, a senior officer of the royal household and the court's original responsibility was for discipline within the royal household. The court had jurisdiction for an area of 12 miles round Westminster, excepting the City of London. In theory, at least one party in each case had to be a member of the royal household; however the prison keepers repeatedly acted improperly, firstly by exercising powers of arrest and detention they did not hold and secondly doing so against people who were not members of the royal household. The prison is first heard of in Southwark in the late 14th century.

The King's Bench was also a royal court, which tried cases requiring royal authority. The court moved with the royal household and originally its prisoners moved with it although, like its near relation the Marshalsea, it acquired a permanent home in Southwark in the late 14th century. As well as housing felons and debtors, in the mid 16th century both the Marshalsea and the King's Bench were used to confine religious prisoners during the religious upheavals of the Reformation.

Conditions in both prisons were notoriously overcrowded, insanitary and cruel and the regimes operating them were corrupt and negligent. Reports of false imprisonment, either without charge or after an order of release had been made, of exorbitant fees, refusal of bail, appalling overcrowding, insanitary conditions and torture were common throughout much of their history.

Such injustices and brutality clearly fed resentment, and resentment festered and grew among many already disposed to violence and who had little respect for authority. It is no surprise therefore that the leaders of the two great national rebellions of the middle ages, the 1381 Peasants' Revolt and Jack Cade's rebellion of 1450 made for the Marshalsea and King's Bench prisons in an attempt to augment their support from those with a specific grudge against the Crown or, as happened in 1450, to release prisoners, so adding to the confusion and disorder.

London Bridge and the Bridge House

Much of the medieval period was characterised by the City of London attempting to gain administrative control over what it saw as its unruly neighbour at the south end of London Bridge. What the City did control and have responsibility for was the very thing that joined the two communities: the bridge itself. A stone bridge was constructed under the oversight of Peter de Colechurch in 1176-1209 and was the first truly permanent link between the north and south banks of the river. The bridge met the southern shore close to the point of its Roman predecessor i.e. about 75 m downstream of the modern bridge.

The Bridge House and Yard, 1827.
The Bridge House and yard were owned by the City of London and were for the operation and repair of London Bridge. It was located near the bridge foot, north of Tooley Street. The function is referred to in the modern name of Bridge Yard, off Tooley Street.

This site is marked by a plaque on the riverfront at the Cotton's Centre. The southern abutment was built c. 1190. The road was elevated on a support of chalk and clay and the river's edge was made secure by a shield of masonry behind which was a mortar core on a timber base. The southern abutment was enlarged in 1445-1460 during a major repair campaign. As well as houses, which were a feature from its earliest days, there was a drawbridge on the south side, raised each evening and at times of national emergency and a chapel dedicated to St Thomas the Martyr. The drawbridge was the site for displaying the decapitated heads of executed traitors and villains, a practice that did not stop until 1661, and there was also a publicly visible cage, or lock up; both demonstrations of the punitive power of the Crown and the City. Under the bridge were waterworks and tidal water wheels.

Maintenance of the bridge was paid for by a fund of money held by, but separate from, the City's core finances. This fund of money from property owned by the City was called the Bridge House Estate. In addition the City had the maintenance yard for the upkeep of the bridge in Southwark. Called the Bridge House, it was near the riverfront to the east of the junction of the high street and Tooley Street. This yard was also used as a grain store for the City, and during the 17th and 18th centuries, the site was increasingly used for warehousing foodstuffs. The City still owns land in Southwark, such as the office block Colechurch House at the foot of London Bridge.

Population, economy and society

It is difficult to establish accurate population figures for the medieval period. The sources available are hard to interpret, often contradictory or incomplete and rarely form a series over time. The task is made even more difficult as this book discusses an area that has no clear administrative boundaries and which had many temporary residents. Therefore evidence must be gathered from sources that at best reflect population trends, such as the erection of new buildings or income from property, or tax returns, and so any conclusions will be open to debate and uncertainty.

It has been calculated that at the start of the medieval period it is likely that Southwark's population was no more than a few hundred, settled around the bridge head and possibly along the northern part of the high street. As in London, Southwark's population grew strongly in the 12th and 13th centuries and possibly reached about 5,000 by 1300. Thus

Southwark's population was approximately 5% of that of London. The population of the area of this book was probably 70% - 80% of this figure. Southwark, along with all areas of England, saw a major fall in population in the mid-14th century as a result of famine and disease, commonly known as the Black Death. Although it is difficult to interpret, the 1381 poll tax return is an important source about population. There is much uncertainty about its completeness and about how to estimate the numbers that were not required to contribute – such as clerics, children, prisoners, or temporary residents in their town houses and the inns, those too poor to be assessed and those that managed to evade payment with, or without, the connivance of the collectors. Once these factors have been accommodated the population of Southwark as a whole has been calculated at approximately 2,000, and so that of our area at 70% - 80% of this figure.

All the available evidence – new streets, cemeteries and numbers of communicants in churches – point to a rapid recovery in population in the generations following the Black Death. By the mid 16th century, Southwark's population is thought to have been approximately 8,500.

As with the population of London, this growth was sustained by immigration, rather than by a surplus of births over deaths. Immigrants were attracted to Southwark by the availability of both work and cheaper rents for housing and business and also by laxer controls on trade than in the City of London. These factors contributed to the significantly greater rate of increase in Southwark's population compared to that of London. By the mid 16th century Southwark was the fourth wealthiest town in the home counties (after London, Canterbury and Reading), was ranked in the top dozen wealthiest towns in England and in the early 17th century was the second most populous area in England after London.

The majority of Southwark's population came from London and nearby counties, but the Borough was also home to a large group of overseas immigrants. These were called the Doche and were Germans or Flemings from the low countries. Many came to England in the 1330s on the invitation of Edward III, who was keen to use their skills as cloth weavers. Southwark's Flemings had a wide range of occupations with an emphasis towards the clothing and decorative trades. In later centuries they diversified into brewing and ale house keeping, occupations where the Borough offered many opportunities. They tended to live, marry and work as a group, the majority living in St Olave's parish. They seem to have been accepted and treated fairly by both their neighbours and by administrators, but were subject to attack by Londoners and by other marauding groups. Southwark's Flemings were massacred in 1381 during the Peasants' Revolt and again in 1470 during an attack on London by the Earl of Warwick, a rival to Edward IV. Their numbers are difficult to establish; by the mid-16th century it was probably in the high hundreds, or about 10% of the total population.

Just as the Borough's population developed in a way that was different to London's, so its occupational structure was very different. Right through the medieval period, the single biggest group (between 25% and 40%) of known occupations was concerned with the making and distribution of food and drink. This is of little surprise: the production and distribution of food and drink was labour intensive and in the inns and townhouses there was a large, ready market of those unable or unwilling to prepare their own food. Brewing was particularly well represented, establishing a tradition that was to continue into the 20th century.

Another occupational group that was disproportionately highly represented were metalworkers, especially smiths, and farriers, who had ready business with the numerous horses bringing travellers to and from Southwark. Another occupation to stand out was leather workers. (Leather working and tanning was later to become a major industry in the neighbouring district of Bermondsey.)

Those active in making and preparing food had two main outlets, the inns and the town's markets. There were two markets. One was regulated by the Great Liberty manor and took place on Wednesdays, Fridays and Saturdays in the open streets near St Thomas' Hospital. The other was under the control of the Guildable manor and took place until mid-afternoon on Wednesdays and Fridays on stalls in the high street immediately south of the bridge. This came under the City's control in 1406. (Control of the main Southwark market was one of the City's key ambitions during the City's gradual accumulation of power over Southwark during the medieval period.) When the City obtained control of the other manors in 1550, the market expanded south along the high street and increased the days it operated to include Mondays and Saturdays inevitably increasing the congestion caused to travellers and traffic.

The market's arrangements required considerable oversight. The authorities needed constant vigilance to ensure goods were of proper quality, that prices were those approved by the market authorities, that weights were accurate, that the street was not unduly blocked by illegal stalls, and that the central gutter was kept clear to maintain a semblance of hygiene. Illegal traders persistently attracted the authorities' attention, notably the innkeepers, who took advantage of the space offered by the inn yard to sell goods, often at inflated prices. The market's expansion over time and space and the continued attempts at illegal trading point to the Borough's thriving and vibrant economy. It is apparent that not only did the markets serve local permanent and temporary residents but they were also an important source of goods for Londoners.

The market was certainly a lively affair, but was tame in comparison to Southwark's annual fair, one of the great entertainments and spectacles of southern England. The Crown first granted the City permission to hold a fair in Southwark in 1444. The fair was to last three days, from 7-9 September. It was held along the full length of the high street and in side streets and inn yards. In addition to food sellers there were entertainments and other distractions. In the 17th and 18th centuries, it was notoriously brash and vulgar.

Manors, landholding and administration
The origin and development of early-medieval Southwark's landowning, legal, judicial, administrative, manorial and parochial structures is very difficult to establish with certainty.

The most important unit of administration and land was the manor. This was an inter-relationship of a landholder (the lord), the group of people who held land from the lord, and the set of laws and customs by which they lived. The manor was administered by manorial officials and a court for settling civil and minor criminal disputes.

It is not fully clear when, how, or under whose authority Southwark's manorial boundaries or lordships evolved. Domesday Book, the great inventory of land and property compiled by William the Conqueror's officials in 1086, offers no firm pointers. From it we can tentatively suggest that in the 11th and 12th centuries, the Crown had direct influence in Southwark (hardly surprising given the Southwark's strategic military importance) as a landholder and controller of administration and justice, but in later years it passed these powers to the evolving manorial structures.

By the late middle ages there were five Southwark manors: Paris Garden was on the town's western riverfront and was controlled by the Hospitallers; the Clink, or Bishop of Winchester's Manor also fronted the river and was between Paris Garden and London Bridge; the King's Manor, controlled by the Prior of Bermondsey, was to the south of these; the small Guildable Manor straddled the bridgehead, and the much larger Great Liberty Manor extended along the riverfront to the east and south-east down Kent Street and the Old Kent Road. Newington was a separate manor and parish. Newington manor was held by the Prior and Convent of Canterbury. Much of the history of Paris Garden, the Clink and King's Manor has been covered in the companion volume *The Story of Bankside*. The Crown was lord of the Guildable Manor. Apart from this, Southwark, (along with its neighbouring parishes of Lambeth, Newington and Bermondsey), were all controlled by ecclesiastical institutions. Despite this common thread, each manor was determinedly independent with its own laws, customs, court and officials.

Some sources mention a Manor of the Maze, centred on the area of Maze Pond on the site of modern Guy's Hospital. This was never a manor in the proper sense and the origin of this name is uncertain.

Although the manors were self-governing, they were not the only institutions with administrative power in Southwark. There was direct Crown interest in the tolls collected by the royal bailiff and in the two royal prisons, the King's Bench and the Marshalsea. The Crown also appointed the officials who administered the County of Surrey's role in the town. The county was responsible for investigating and trying major felonies and for the coroner. Its responsibilities, exercised through the justices of the peace, grew through the Tudor period to include new duties, such as the oversight of parish administration.

This complex situation led to diversity and inconsistency. The confusion provided an impression of laxity and this was reinforced by the natural independence of each body to represent its own interest. This had two consequences. The first was an inability to co-operate and compromise in order to establish a co-ordinated administration and so petition the Crown for a charter granting self-governing status. The second consequence was to attract the attention of the City of London, which was alarmed at what it perceived as Southwark's lawless nature and a place of refuge for criminals that were wanted to stand trial in the City, and by its economic power and lack of regulation.

In 1325, the City made its first attempt to gain control over Southwark. This failed, but two years later the Crown passed its tax-raising powers in respect of the Guildable Manor over to the City. In 1406 the City gained the power to arrest and try criminals that were wanted in the City but again, only if they were caught in the Guildable Manor. The acquisition of such minor responsibilities and in only a very small part of Southwark did little to make the City any more comfortable about its troublesome neighbour.

In 1550, the City obtained much greater power. This was rather a consequence of Henry VIII's greed, opportunism and vanity than the City winning its case on principle. The years following the Reformation – when England split from the Catholic church based in Rome and when Henry closed down and took control of the assets of the monastic houses – saw a huge renewal in Crown interest in Southwark. Once again Southwark (briefly) became a royal town. Henry VIII acquired the Paris Garden, Clink, Great Liberty and King's Manors, and the Suffolk Place Estate. Suffolk Place was once owned by Charles Brandon, Duke of Suffolk and was on the west side of the high street at its southern end opposite St George's church. Whatever Henry VIII's plans for Southwark might have been, they were abandoned, as in 1550 the Crown sold to the City for £980 land, jurisdiction and rights over the King's Manor and Great Liberty Manor and had its rights over the Guildable Manor confirmed. This gave the Crown much needed income and political support from the City. The City financed the purchase with money from the Bridge House Estate. The purchase meant the City owned these lands and could take rents from them, it could require residents to appear before its courts or serve on juries; it had powers to appoint the coroner, to impose the City's governmental structure based on wards, aldermen and councillors and to hold a market. The City had gained its most extensive control over Southwark, but to its continued frustration its power was limited, as Paris Garden and the Clink Manors were still independent and the Crown retained control over the King's Bench and Marshalsea prisons and over the Suffolk Place Estate. Suffolk Place evolved into the Mint, one of the poorest and most notorious of the town's areas.

The City imposed some of its governmental structures on the town, but never fully integrated it into the City. It exercised its new right to appoint the justices (much to the dislike of the county of Surrey), and St Margaret's church, which was no longer used for worship after the establishment of St Saviour's as the new parish church, was converted to the court house and prison for the areas under the City's jurisdiction. This was the first administrative use of this site, which was later to be used for Southwark's Town Hall. The second action was an attempt to superimpose the City's administrative structure of wards, each electing members to the Court of Common Council and Court of Aldermen. A new ward was created, Bridge Ward Without. However, Bridge Ward Without was as semi-detached administratively as it was geographically as its alderman was never elected by the ward, but appointed by the City's existing aldermen. Over time the holder of this position had decreasing contact with the area he was supposed to represent. Equally no provision was made for the election of representatives to the City's other governing body, the Court of Common Council.

By the late 16th century Southwark was an administrative muddle. The City of London, the County of Surrey, the Crown, parochial institutions and manorial institutions all had roles. Their relative influence waxed and waned over time reflecting their shifting enthusiasms and resources. It was a muddle that was not properly sorted out until the beginning of the 20th century.

It is impossible to give a precise date for the end of the medieval period, but three events were significant in shaping the next phase of the Borough's history. They were the Reformation of the 1530s and so the end of the church's role as landowner, administrator and of the temporary residency of senior clerics; the purchase in 1550 by the City of control over the King's and Great Liberty manors and the emergence in the early years of the 17th century of the parish as the main unit of local government. Physically, however, the town's shape changed little, as no major expansion or other changes took place until well into the 18th century.

CHAPTER 2

The early modern period

The 17th and 18th centuries saw the Borough develop from a ribbon development to an urban one and its southern part became inextricably linked with the northern part of the neighbouring parish of St Mary, Newington. The period saw many of the existing institutions develop and reform to meet the new challenges posed by the town's increased size and population: churches were rebuilt, roads were widened and commercial enterprises multiplied. Genuinely new features were the building of large-scale riverside wharves, especially to the east of London Bridge, and the foundation of Guy's Hospital. The period also offered two opportunities for more radical redevelopment in the response to a number of serious and damaging fires that took place during the late 17th century.

At the same time many existing features retained their earlier character· the prisons held on to and even increased their reputation for corruption and appalling conditions, the fair became even longer, more lively and more of a nuisance and the inns remained the backbone of the town's economy. Administratively the parishes developed as the unit of local government, and at the same time the role of the manor courts diminished. The City of London and County of Surrey still retained the functions they held at the end of the medieval period.

TOWNSCAPE

The Borough's townscape and population changed significantly in the two and a half centuries to 1800. The changes in character were very different to those that took place elsewhere in London. While this period saw the development of London's fashionable west end and the building of the first and grandest mansions and squares in Marylebone and Bloomsbury, the Borough saw quite the opposite, as the town was abandoned by aristocracy and replaced by the urban poor.

Southwark is described in detail by London's first historian John Stow, whose *Survey of London* was published in 1598, but described a London of generations earlier. In the Borough he draws attention to the high street inns, the townhouses of the prelates and nobility, St Saviour's church and the prisons. Other important sources for the Borough's townscape are contemporary drawings. There are numerous panoramas of London and Southwark appears in the foreground to many. The

Visscher view of 1616 is the most notable in this respect. However the high street is shown in even more detail in Wyngaerde's view of c. 1550.

The events most symbolic of the Borough's transition into the early modern period was the disappearance, during the late 16th century and early 17th centuries, of the townhouses of the medieval aristocracy; their owners' loyalty to Southwark overwhelmed by the town's urbanisation and the commercialism of the inns. In many cases the buildings fell into disrepair, were demolished and replaced with smaller tenements.

Properties previously owned or occupied by the Cobham and Ponyngs families became inns or beer houses and the inn of Lord Ferrers became a burial ground. Properties still owned by monastic houses at the time of the Reformation changed ownership as a result of their dissolution. Many were converted into private dwellings; some were occupied by their new secular owners, while others were leased out. For example, the convent buildings of the Priory of St Mary Overie became the town house of Sir Anthony Brown, Master of the King's Horse. On Bankside, Winchester Palace, the townhouse of the Bishop of Winchester, was not used as his private accommodation after 1626. Fastolf Place on Tooley Street changed hands many times during the 16th century and the house and its grounds gradually gave way to warehouses.

Suffolk Place, the sumptuous house and grounds at the corner of Borough High Street opposite St George's church, was the home until the 1530s of the Brandon family, later Dukes of Suffolk. It changed hands frequently thereafter, briefly becoming a Royal Mint (hence Mint Street and the surrounding area of the same name) until its demolition in 1562. By the late 17th century, the site was partly covered by small houses and this process continued after 1702 when Thomas Lant took possession of the land, started to redevelop existing properties and built on much of the remaining open land. The Mint also had the dubious distinction of sustaining Southwark and the Borough's reputation of lawlessness. It was not until 1723 that it became subject to the same regime of law enforcement as the rest of the area.

Development was generally piecemeal across the whole of the Borough, new building taking place as and when a landowner had the finance and motivation to undertake a refurbishment, rebuild or a new development. However, in the 1660s and 1670s the town as a whole had major opportunities to upgrade its buildings and even redesign the street layout. These opportunities came as a result of a series of fires in the late 17th century. While none were as destructive as London's great fire of 1666, all caused significant damage.

Fires

Fire was a persistent hazard in urban areas at this time. Buildings were usually made with significant amounts of wood and roofed with thatch. In the period before safety matches the common way of lighting a new fire was from a bucket of smouldering coals; during darkness domestic lighting was by candles. In addition the Borough's (temporary) population of inn dwellers probably did not take as much care as they might have done in their own property. For some, the effects of Southwark's famous ale would have further compromised their prudence. Once a building caught alight, there was no organised fire fighting force and water supplies were weak and irregular. The only effective way of preventing the fire from spreading was the drastic one of blowing up properties in its path, so creating a gap across which the fire could not jump.

There are records of fires in 1667, 1670, 1676 and 1689. Samuel Pepys records a 'great fire' in Southwark in April 1667, which was visible from the north side of the river and of seeing an engine playing water onto it until it was put out. The fire of 1670 destroyed the George Inn and all its outbuildings. The George was swiftly rebuilt but again became a casualty of fire in the high street's most destructive conflagration in May 1676. This started in and spread rapidly from an oil shop situated between the George and the Talbot inns. It destroyed numerous houses (one source suggests 600, which seems implausibly high) and, while its focus of destruction was on the northern part of the high street, it caused damage as far south as St George's church. It burned for 16 hours and claimed 20 lives. It destroyed six of the most important Borough inns: the George, the Queen's Head, the Talbot, the White Hart, the Green Dragon and the King's Head. It also destroyed the old St Margaret's church, at that time used as a court house by the City of London for the parts of Southwark it administered. The fire of September 1689 started opposite the King's Bench Prison at the southern end of the high street. It damaged part of that prison, the Falcon and Half Moon Inns and nearly 200 houses.

Two features stand out from this spate of fires and their reporting. The first is the extent to which the inns are mentioned when detailing damage to buildings, so reinforcing to us their size, status and economic importance to the town. The second is that when rebuilding took place, and particularly rebuilding of the inns, it was substantially on a like-for-like basis, using known building techniques and traditional materials that were easy to obtain. A rapid return to normal business was more important than architectural innovation or radical town planning. The only example of an important new building was a municipal one, the replacement of St Margaret's church by Southwark's first town hall, built by the City of London and open for business in 1689. This made good use of its prominent site at the fork in the high street at the junction with Counter Lane.

Roads

More significant changes to the Borough's layout and to the size and composition of its population were those brought about as a result of the building of new bridges across the Thames and the laying out of new roads to serve them. While the most dramatic changes were to the west and the south of the Borough, where new roads were built to serve new bridges at Blackfriars, Westminster, Lambeth and later Waterloo, there was inevitably a need to link the Borough directly with these new roads. The building of Blackfriars Bridge presented the residents and businesses of Borough High Street with a quandary. While the reduced traffic congestion would doubtless have been welcome, there would also have been an anxiety that fewer travellers would reduce business. One of the early plans was for a new road to run parallel to the river to connect Blackfriars Road from a point near its north end with Borough High Street near the town hall. It was never built and instead Union Street, the eastern portion of which was laid out in 1781, gradually extended west to Blackfriars Road.

Churches

St Saviour's church dominated Southwark's parochial scene, indeed it was one of the largest parish churches in the London area. It was also a parish controlled by its parishioners, rather than under the patronage of a lord of the manor, or a distant institution. In 1614, the parishioners bought the church outright and gained the right to appoint their own clergy. While this period saw no major changes to the structure of the church, the interior was enhanced by a number of memorials to the great and good of the parish. The largest is to Alderman William Humble (died 1616) and his two wives. Nearby is the memorial to Launcelot Andrewes (died 1626), the last Bishop of Winchester to live in the palace next door. Other memorials are to William Emerson (died 1575); John Trehearne (died 1618); John Bingham (died 1625) and Lionel Lockyer (died 1672).

The original medieval building of the church of St George the Martyr survived into the early modern period, but there are no reliably accurate views of it. The church is shown in the Wyngaerde panorama of c.1550 and the new one, without the top of its tower, in Hogarth's engraving of Southwark Fair of c. 1733.

It is clear that by the early 17th century the original medieval building was in a poor state of repair. Extensive work was carried out to the steeple, the gallery and the pews and a new aisle was built to the north side, so enlarging the church and diminishing the size of the churchyard. Despite these improvements there were conflicting accounts a century later of its state of repair. While in 1715 the church was described in approving terms, only fifteen years later there were complaints that it was too dangerous to enter. The latter plea was well-timed, as it coincided with a church building programme by the Anglican Church (and overseen by the Commissioners for the Building of Fifty New Churches). The commissioners were sympathetic to St George's vulnerable situation and granted £6,000 for a new building. The medieval church was torn down, the foundation stone of the new building laid in 1734 and it was completed two years later. The new building was designed by John Price. The building has the unusual distinction of a parish boundary marker on the fabric of the church, as the southern wall of the church is part of the boundary with St Mary, Newington.

The main body of the church is made from brick with Portland stone edgings and tower. Internally there are galleries on three sides. The organ, the bells and the coat of arms of Kings James I and Charles I were in the medieval church and the font is a copy of the one from the medieval church.

The church was, of course, a place of burial, both in its crypt and in its churchyard. By the early 19th century the crypt and churchyard were full and the churchyard was extended to the north and so became a neighbour of the Marshalsea Prison.

In 1702 St Thomas's church was rebuilt.

St Olave's church underwent frequent refurbishment and repairs during the 17th century but despite these, by the early 18th century it was in a poor state of repair, its fabric suffering from occasional floods from the Thames. The medieval church collapsed in 1738 and in 1740 a substantially new and larger building was erected under the supervision of Henry Flitcroft.

The period also saw a growth in non-conformist places of worship. Southwark was known as a place for religious radicalism. Many radicals were locked up in its prisons, and this contact led to further radicalisation. For example, John Greenwood and Henry Barrowe, while imprisoned in the Clink, set up their own church. In the 17th century what evolved

St Olave's church, 1830.

into the Pilgrim Fathers' Memorial church was established. It met at Deadman's Place and in the late 18th century moved to Union Street. It is likely that some of the earliest settlers in north America were from its congregation; they were attracted to the New World by the freedom it gave them to worship as they wished.

John Harvard was amongst those that went to America. Harvard's family was part of the town's elite and owned the Queen's Head on the high street. John had been christened in St Saviour's and attended the grammar school. He and his wife Ann left for America in 1637. The reasons are unclear: it could have been for religious reasons, or from fear of plague (he had just lost close relatives in an outbreak) or following a pioneering instinct. He was a man of considerable learning and he took his book collection with him. He settled near Boston and soon became one of the leaders of the new colony. John Harvard died only a year after his arrival, but his will still provides benefit to the people of America today as he left half his wealth and all his library to establish a place of learning. This has evolved into the mighty Harvard University in Massachusetts. His life and this endowment are commemorated in a chapel in Southwark cathedral.

A striking feature of the Borough by 1800 was the number of burial grounds. In addition to their churchyards, St Saviour, St Olave and St George the Martyr all had additional grounds. St Olave had one on the south side of Tooley Street (now under Station Approach) and St Saviour's one at the junction of Red Cross Street and Union Street. (This is also known as the Cross Bones burial ground, where, reputedly, although without much evidence other than probability, the Bankside prostitutes were buried. The public interest caused by its excavation during the archaeology preceding the building of the Jubilee Line extension made it a local cause celebre with calls for its preservation and restrictions on building on the currently vacant site.) St George's had an additional burial ground at the south end of Great Dover Street, which it opened in 1711 and enlarged in 1744. St Thomas' burial ground was opposite the church on the south side of St Thomas's Street. There were two burial grounds to the east of the original buildings of Guy's Hospital (both now under Guy's Tower), one of which was used by St Thomas' Hospital. Guy's and St Thomas' Hospitals had a joint burial ground at the south side of Snowsfields and under the modern Lockyer Estate.

St Thomas' church, 1814.
The church was central and integral to the hospital. It was rebuilt in 1702.

Prisons, courts and the Town Hall

Through the 17th and 18th centuries the prisons remained an important feature of the Borough. Between 1580 and 1750 three of the prisons, the Marshalsea, the King's Bench and the County Gaol were near neighbours on a stretch of the high street no more than 150 m long.

The Marshalsea's function was defined in the 17th century when it assumed the role of a debtors' prison, a role it retained until its closure in 1842. From the 17th century it was also used to imprison those convicted by the Admiralty courts – the Admiralty is the government body that oversaw the Royal Navy. Until the early 19th century, the prison was in premises on the east side of the high street, just north of the modern Mermaid Court.

Until the middle of the 18th century, the King's Bench prison was the Marshalsea's near neighbour on the east side of Borough High Street, just north of Angel Place on the site of the modern number 199. In 1758, it moved to purpose-built premises in St George's Fields. Despite its initially isolated position, the prison was the focus for disturbances. There was violence when John Wilkes, the opportunistic, charismatic radical, was imprisoned there in 1768 and again in 1780 during the Gordon Riots, when it was partly burnt. The prisoners generally enjoyed a relaxed regime as those that paid the requisite fee were permitted through a system called the Rules, to live, work and associate freely within a defined area in the vicinity of the prison.

In the 17th and early 18th centuries, prison conditions and administration had scarcely improved on earlier generations. The prisons were overcrowded, insanitary, brutal, corrupt and unjust. False imprisonment was common as was torture. In the King's Bench 80 prisoners were reported to have died of starvation in the year 1624 alone.

Southwark's peaceable residents might have looked on these institutions with a mixture of curiosity and dread. Dread at the possibility of any escape of the brutalised inmates, so suppressing any scruples they might have had about the nature of the regimes that kept their near neighbours from coming no nearer.

Southwark was the largest town in Surrey, so it was appropriate that the county should choose it as a site for its prison. Like the royal prisons, the institution was run by its keeper for profit and prisoners were housed in converted premises; in this case an inn called the White Lion.

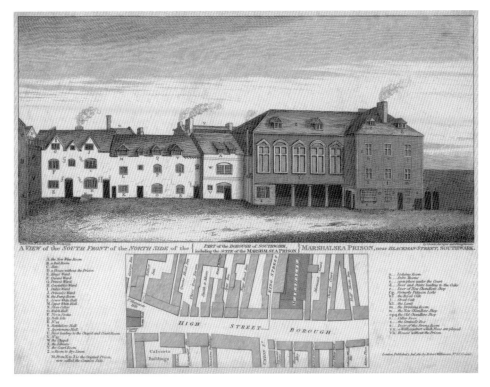

Marshalsea Prison, Borough High Street, c1811.
The prison occupied this site, just north of Mermaid Court, until 1811, when it moved 100 m to the south. The helpful key identifies the grandly-named King's, Queen's and similar wards in the whitewashed gabled building on the left and the court room above the colonnade on the right.

It is first heard of in 1580. This too was on the east side of the high street, just north of St George's church. A separate but related Surrey House of Correction came into existence by the middle of the 17th century. In 1773 the House of Correction moved to new premises on the west side of Newington Causeway. In the 1790s the county moved its gaol to purpose-built premises at Horsemonger Lane in Newington, near the junction of Newington Causeway and Harper Road. These premises housed both a gaol and a court. They were designed by local architect George Gwilt and had capacity for 400 prisoners.

The final prison, the Borough Compter, also contained a court house. It was run by the City of London and was used as the court house and prison for local cases that came under the jurisdiction of the City of London. The site was also used for other aspects of the City's administration of Southwark. The name Compter is a corruption of counter i.e. a keeper of records. In its early days the court and its prison were in St Margaret's church. The prison was enlarged in 1609, but destroyed by the fire of 1676. The replacement, which also included the court and prison, was Southwark's first purpose-built town hall. The court house was used for the trial of those involved in the Scottish rebellion of 1745. The building was burned by the Gordon Rioters in 1780 and replaced in 1793 by a new town hall.

The Town Hall, c.1790.
The Borough's town hall, from which the City of London administered its responsibilities in Southwark. Note the City's coat of arms.

PEOPLE AND SOCIETY

Population and social structure

The population of the Borough grew perhaps three or fourfold over this period from maybe 8,500 in 1550 to about 30,000 in 1800. Precise figures are extremely difficult to establish due to the lack of sources that record population, or from which population can be accurately calculated. The exercise is made even harder as this book discusses areas that cut across parish boundaries.

We can be certain that the Borough was by-passed by the growing power, glamour and social prestige that was prevalent elsewhere in London. Political activity focused on Westminster, legal activity on the Inns of Court and the aristocracy and the cultural elite on the West End.

The Borough, as ever, was a destination for newcomers to London, indeed the area's, and London's, population grew only because of sustained migration to the metropolis. The Borough offered cheap accommodation and access to casual work. Most immigrants came from the English home counties, but maybe 10% of the population was Irish. The population was not exclusively white, especially in the 18th century. Black men and women, many possibly slaves, who were landed at riverside wharves, would have been a relatively common sight. There is a record in the St Olave's parish register of 1770 of a marriage between Michael Thomas, a black man and Ann Bradley. This encouraging evidence of multi-culturalism is marred by a report in the *Gentleman's Magazine* of a violent interruption to the service by a press gang, though their motive is unclear from the report.

Socially the town was extremely mixed. The inn keepers, the wharf owners and the senior medical staff at the hospitals were at its social and economic pinnacle. Thereafter came shop keepers and those running small businesses. After them the social scale fell away rapidly reaching a nadir in the unfortunate and unwholesome residents and staff of the prisons.

Adminstration

The Borough's administration was an exceedingly complex affair. Numerous bodies had a role in providing and overseeing justice, public protection, social welfare and other services. There were four main participants: the parishes, the City of London, Surrey County and the Crown.

Each parish was responsible for its own civil as well as ecclesiastical affairs and over this period their civil responsibilities grew. There were five parishes: four in Southwark proper: St Saviour (whose vestry was known as the Corporation of Wardens of St Saviour), St Olave, St Thomas and St George the Martyr, and St Mary, Newington. Their principal responsibility was for the poor law (exercised by officials called overseers of the poor) and other responsibilities included highways and the parish watch – a proto police force. They also oversaw parochial charities and the bodies founded by them, most commonly schools and almshouses and other welfare facilities for the old or infirm. The unit of parochial administration was also known as the vestry.

After 1550 much of Southwark became part of the City of London as in that year the City acquired the rights of manorial administration previously held by the Guildable, King's and Great Liberty manors. The area the City had rights over included all of the parishes of St George the Martyr, St Saviour and St Olave (but not St Mary, Newington) and so included both sides of the high street and the riverfront east of St Mary Overie dock. The City took on these new powers and responsibilities only half-heartedly. The City's administrative structures were never fully implemented and the new powers only intermittently used. These new powers included overseeing the market (until 1756), regulating trade, notably granting licences to victuallers, dealing with petty criminal cases, and dealing with breaches of local bye-laws. Other functions included maintaining London Bridge, and St Thomas' Hospital.

The County of Surrey had two main roles: command over military affairs (it was therefore responsible for raising a militia when men were needed for military service) and, through the justices of the peace, the oversight of parochial administration. The county also had its own court and prison in Southwark.

The Crown and parliament maintained the Marshalsea and King's Bench Prisons and retained (but hardly exercised) control over the Suffolk Place Estate. Because of this lax attention to justice the Mint was a haven for criminals. Parliament also gave authority for major public works, such as the building of new roads, through local Acts of Parliament.

Poor relief
A major function of the vestry was to provide for the poor of its parish. It did this through grants of clothes, fuel or money, by finding employers for those needing work, or by taking people into its workhouse. Funds

to pay for this care were raised from a property tax called the rate, collected from property in that parish alone, so each parish had to fund its own provision. Much of the parishes' work was establishing if those applying for help qualified for it, and rejecting those who didn't. To qualify one had to have been born there or had been authorised to settle. Visitors, or temporary residents were not welcome, nor were pregnant women about to give birth. Those not entitled to relief were sent back to their place of origin. The number of these removal orders is evidence for the huge economic pull of London and Southwark, they tell us a great deal about the places from which people migrated, and they contain personal and often deeply moving stories of hope, need and rejection.

The poor law regime was a strict one and distinguished between the deserving and the undeserving poor. Relief could be given in the form of money, food, fuel or clothes. Poor children could be apprenticed to learn a trade. There are many surviving apprenticeship indentures for St George the Martyr and St Mary, Newington parishes. Sometimes this was with local firms, but, as provincial towns became industrialised, it was with distant employers looking for cheap labour. Often this was a large-scale enterprise. One letter of about 1790 addressed to St George the Martyr from a firm in Cheshire set out a 'plan for disposing of 200 parish children'. It says *"we take them at 9 or 10 years old... they labour from 6am to 7pm in summer and from 7am to 8pm in winter. In the evening after work they wash, get their suppers and go to school, from thence to bed."*

The poor, but most often the sick, or aged poor, could be admitted to the parish workhouse. St George's was in Mint Street. This was built in 1732 and rebuilt in 1782, the St Saviour's workhouse was on what became Southwark Bridge Road. St Olave's workhouse was in Parish Street, Bermondsey.

Charities and schools
A major feature of post-Reformation life, and one that continued in similar fashion until the 18th century, was the establishment of parochial charities funded through bequests left by residents. Many of the town's important social, educational and welfare institutions had their origins in benefactions of this sort.

Schools established in this way included St Saviour's parochial school, founded in 1681 when Mrs Dorothy Applebee gave £20 to establish a free school in St Saviour's parish. This originally met in the churchyard and later moved to Union Street. It has evolved into the Cathedral School of St Saviour and St Mary Overie.

A charity school stood at the corner of Red Cross Street and Union Street. Twenty children were educated and clothed by the benefaction of Mrs Elizabeth Newcomen, or Newcombe, in her will of 1674, and seventy by the will of John Collet of 1711. The building in this place was erected in 1713 after Mr Collet's benefaction was received. A charity school was established in 1781, next to Guy's Hospital, for thirty boys. St George's parochial school was founded in 1698 to provide schooling for 40 boys. In 1747 a girls' school was established. In St Olave's parish a charity school for about fifty girls was supported by voluntary contributions.

In addition to these schools was the establishment of two grammar schools. One was associated with St Saviour's parish and it received its Royal Charter in 1562 and the other with St Olave's; it was established in 1571. St Saviour's School was in Green Dragon Court until it was burnt by the fire of 1676. It was rebuilt nearby but was forced to move to Sumner Street in 1839 to accommodate an expansion of the market. Its educational and governance arrangements were based on St Paul's School, and it offered an overwhelmingly classical curriculum.

Charitable bequests were also used to establish almshouses. Examples include Cure's College for sixteen poor parishioners, founded in 1584 by Thomas Cure, saddler to the queen. Edward Alleyn established almshouses in 1616 for ten men and women; later, at Dulwich, he founded an almshouse and a school. Henry Jackson founded an almshouse in 1660 for two poor women. There were almshouses in St. Thomas' Street belonging to that parish.

Numerous institutions with a London-wide scope and aimed at helping particular groups were established in St George's Fields in the late 18th century; examples include the Bethlem Hospital and the Philanthropic Society (see *The Story of Bankside* for further details). The Asylum for the Deaf and Dumb in Kent Street was of similar character. This was started by the Rev John Townsend and the Rev Henry Cox Mason in 1792.

Public health
Despite this growing provision of charitable and social care, these bodies were able to contribute little to solving the health needs and problems of the average resident of the Borough. The biggest threats to good health were from diseases that had no known origin or cure and for which even treatment was rudimentary. The most feared and the most dramatic was plague. This had been a persistent visitor to London since

the middle ages. It is of course best known for its catastrophic (and last) outbreak in 1665, but was responsible for many deaths in earlier centuries. It was particularly feared because it struck seemingly randomly and its causes were entirely unknown. Plague also hit hardest in London's suburbs, such as Southwark. There houses were often poorly built, more crowded, the population poorer and badly nourished. Most importantly, they did not benefit from the City's attempts to control the spread of the disease through isolation of victims and those who had been in contact with them. The other problem was endemic disease, specially, smallpox, typhus and tuberculosis, which particularly affected infants.

A further hazard, especially prevalent in the early 18th century, was gin. Cheap, easily available, as readily consumed by women as men, and potent, it was the drink of choice for those wishing, or needing, to blot out their immediate surroundings.

Guy's Hospital

Today, the Borough's single biggest institution is Guy's Hospital. By the standards of London's oldest hospitals, such as St Thomas' and St Bartholomew's, Guy's is a modern institution and grew partly in response to the neighbouring St Thomas' Hospital's unwillingness to treat certain groups of patients. Since it opened in 1725 it has grown hugely.

The hospital is named after its founder and benefactor, Thomas Guy. Guy was born in Southwark. He was a successful businessman and politician and for much of his life he had been both a governor and benefactor of St Thomas' Hospital. The hospital was founded to both complement and supplement the work of its long-established neighbour. It was to provide both care to those St Thomas' might consider too sick to treat and also treatment for the ordinary sick. The original benefaction also allowed for the care of lunatics. In 1721, when Guy was aged 77, he obtained from St Thomas' some land on the south side of St Thomas' Street and the first building, a rectangle enclosing two open areas, was erected. It provided space for 100 beds. This building still survives today and is called Old Guy's House.

In the late 1730s, Guy's Hospital obtained the land between its north front at St Thomas' Street and a new wing, the east wing (the site of the modern Boland House), was added. The original east wing was destroyed in World War II and rebuilt thereafter. Its opposite pair, the west wing, was added in 1774. This contains the chapel in which there is both a memorial and the remains of Thomas Guy, which were placed there in 1780. The courtyard formed by the wings contains a statue of Thomas Guy, which was erected in 1739.

Expansion to the south started in 1744 when the governors obtained land on which they built a lunatic asylum. Further land to the south was obtained in the early 19th century and so keen was the hospital to expand that, in the first instance, the existing warehouses were used to house sick beds.

Guy's attracted distinguished doctors who both treated patients and taught in the medical school it ran in conjunction with St Thomas'. They included Richard Bright, Thomas Addison and Thomas Hodgkin, all of whom had the diseases they discovered named after them. Bright worked on diseases of the kidneys, Addision of the glands near the kidneys and Hodgkin of the lymph glands and spleen. The surgeon Astley Cooper both taught in the medical school and was a pioneer in surgery of veins and circulation. Guy's was also the first hospital to appoint a dental surgeon (it did so in 1799) and dentistry still plays a central role in the hospital's functions.

Probably the most famous person to be associated with Guy's isn't known in a medical context at all. This was the poet John Keats. He trained there as an apothecary in 1815-1816, but never went on to work in a medical capacity.

The foundation of Guy's Hospital was in keeping with the wider context of events elsewhere in London, as the second quarter of the 18th century was an unusually fertile time for London hospitals. At this time Westminster, St George's, the London and the Middlesex (all general hospitals) were established, other ancient institutions rebuilt and specialist hospitals also founded. In another sense it was the passing of an era, because Guy's was one of the last examples of the initiative and benefaction of one man. This form of individual charitable giving looked back to the 17th century, rather than forward to the 18th, when charitable bodies were more often founded through co-operative public subscription.

St Thomas' Hospital
In the middle ages St Thomas' was an ecclesiastical institution and was closed down at the dissolution of the religious houses in the 1530s. Edward VI refounded it in 1551 and passed control to the City of

St Thomas'
Hospital, 1758.
A view east from the
high street, showing
the three new courts
built 1693–1709.

London. At the same time it was rededicated to St Thomas the Apostle. The governors were representatives of the City and they appointed its officers: steward, treasurer, hospitaller (who dealt with appointments), surgeons and a matron. In the early 17th century it had fewer than 300 patients, who went through strict criteria for admission and then were subject to an equally strict regime. It was hit financially by the Great Fire of London, as many of the properties it owned were damaged, reducing its income from their rental. It was damaged in the Southwark fires of 1676 and 1681 and was substantially rebuilt 1693-1709. This was largely due to the efforts of its president, Robert Clayton. Three new courts were built on an east-west axis.

Other health care

Guy's and St Thomas' were not the only hospitals in the Borough as at its eastern end was the Lock Hospital. This was on the site of the modern Bricklayers' Arms road junction of the Old Kent Road with Great Dover Street and the New Kent Road. The Lock Hospital was a medieval foundation for the treatment of leprosy and which in the 18th century treated those with venereal diseases. It was closed in 1760.

Founded nearby, at the junction of Great Dover Street and Swan Street 17 years later, was the Surrey Dispensary. This was established to provide medicines to the sick and midwifery services to those giving birth at home.

ECONOMY, INDUSTRY, COMMERCE AND TRADE

Inns

The Borough's main economic function was as a place of communications and trade. The inns were central to this. Until 1750 London Bridge was the only bridge over the Thames and until 1769, when Blackfriars Bridge was opened, it was the only entry point into the City. Additionally, London Bridge's drawbridge and gates could prevent entry to or exit from the City as and when the City authorities chose. The gates were not removed until the late 1750s. These factors maintained a demand for the Borough inns, which provided temporary accommodation, food and stabling. The demand for travel to London also expanded in the 17th and 18th centuries as London's status and power grew. It has been estimated that in the early 18th century there were about 200 inns in London and that around two dozen of these were off Borough High Street. The inns were major enterprises, typically with a small frontage to the high street and a yard behind with buildings on one or both sides extending back for 100m or more. The inns combined the functions of modern hotels, transport termini and garages in one. They were on both sides of the high street and the highest concentration was in the section north of St George's church. They have left an indelible mark on the road layout of the Borough, which still has numerous alleys running from it. Some inns had a particular penchant for animal names: the Falcon, the Boar's Head, the White Horse, the Greyhound, the Red Lion and the White Hart. Others attempted to put more human and even royal prestige in their name: the King's Head, the Queen's Head, the George, the Spur and the Tabard or Talbot.

The River Thames

Growing riverside trade was increasingly important to the Borough's economy. London was indisputably the nation's most important port and as overseas power grew so did the amount, variety and value of goods imported. Many of the imported raw materials were processed in London and then re-exported to continental Europe. It has been estimated that in the 18th century, London handled 70% of England's trade by value. Goods could, however, only be landed at the so-called legal quays, which were on the north bank of the Thames and downstream of London Bridge. The increase in trade caused huge congestion on the river and, until there was space, ships had to wait mid-stream or at so-called sufferance wharves. This unsatisfactory situation led to a campaign for the building of cut inland docks and later, the use of wharves for unloading overseas trade. The expansion of trade in the 18th century saw a corresponding growth in riverside warehouse capacity and by 1750 the areas on either side of London Bridge were built up in this way. The biggest player in the warehousing and later wharfing downstream of London Bridge was the Hay's Wharf Company, which was founded in 1651.

Not all goods travelled by river. One distinctive commodity that arrived by road was hops. These were stored in warehouses, especially to the east of the high street and were used in local breweries, such as the Anchor on Bankside and the Black Horse at Maze Pond.

Other activities included tenter grounds, where cloth was stretched on the ground to dry after washing and dyeing. There was also a major Delftware pottery adjacent to St Saviour's church.

Borough Market

While the Thames provided the means to import and distribute goods to England and London, the Borough's retail and domestic trade was carried on in the town's market. This was held three days a week in the high street and stretched as far south as the town hall on the west side of the road and the Swan inn on the east side. The market was a major feature of the town's life, providing a trading and social focus for many of its residents. It was also a noisy, messy and sometimes unwholesome affair. By the early 18th century, it was also hugely disruptive to traffic attempting to use London Bridge. In 1754 the City of London, which ran the market, put the interests of travellers to the City over those of Southwark and petitioned Parliament to permit the market's abolition.

This course of events was unpalatable to the townsfolk and so at the same time the parish officials from St Saviour's obtained permission from Parliament for the market to continue under their control, on a new site away from the road. The trustees bought a piece of land north of St Margaret's Hill between the high street and Counter Lane and were allowed to raise £8,000 to pay for it. This site, still the heart of the modern Borough Market, was first used for trade when the land was finally bought two years later. The market had a dual function, as wholesale and retail, with the changeover signalled at 10.30 am by the ringing of a bell.

A market house was built to give protection to those regulating the traders but there was no permanent cover for the stall holders until 1801. Although no longer trading on the highway, the huge number of vehicles needed to bring goods to market and the visiting customers must have meant any improvements to the congestion levels in the high street were minimal.

While the Borough's main economic role was as a distributor, it also started to develop its own distinctive position in industry and manufacturing. At first this might be surprising given the cost of London land and labour, the relative lack of energy sources (coal had to be shipped in from the north east coalfields) and regulation by the City authorities. Despite these obstacles, printing, glassmaking, pottery, leather working, food, brewing and hatmaking and later engineering all developed as important local activities.

Southwark Fair

Another feature of the life of the Borough, part commercial but chiefly recreational, and also held on the high street was Southwark Fair. While the Borough never became home to one of the fashionable London pleasure grounds that developed in the 18th century, the fair more than put Southwark on London's entertainment map. The fair was held in September each year. While this undoubtedly reached its zenith of popularity in the 18th century, unlike the market, it failed to survive it. Southwark Fair was initially held over a three day period, although by the 18th century it lasted a fortnight. It was one of London's great fairs along with St Bartholomew. It was both a great attraction and a great inconvenience. It attracted the great entertainers of the day: actors (including the leading theatre companies), musicians, magicians, freaks, acrobats and those with all manner of animal shows: bears, horses, dogs and monkeys. These were supported by traders selling all types of refreshments and other goods. For the fortnight, the Borough was turned into a noisy, dirty, drunken, joyous, threatening mass of people, animals, stalls and refuse.

Southwark Fair, c.1733 by William Hogarth.
All the vigour, vulgarity, popularity and hazards of the fair are exposed here. This view is often printed, and displayed back to front. The clock face of St George's church, writing and bagpipe player definitively show this way to be correct.

The fair is recorded by Hogarth's picture *Southwark Fair*, of c. 1733, clearly showing the great performers of the time. Also evident is the throng of people, the competing noise from drums, trumpets and bagpipes, the hazardous structures (a first-floor balcony is shown in mid-collapse) and intense, though not entirely innocent, merry making.

The fair also attracted visitors from all walks of life, from the elites of court, business and society, to urban low life and rural visitors. In the 1660s both Samuel Pepys and John Evelyn visited and described the fair. At the same time members of the Court paid a rare visit to Southwark to see its attractions. Inevitably the fair was also a magnet for petty and not so petty crime, including pickpockets and prostitutes, many of whom would have been home-grown and possibly grateful of a shorter journey than usual to the place where they could exercise their skills and attractions.

In 1763 the fair was suppressed by the City of London and probably the greatest metaphor for Southwark's unruly, independent and boisterous character ended.

CHAPTER 3
The long nineteenth century: 1800-1939

There were huge changes in the Borough in the 140 years after 1800. The population rose to unwholesome and unsustainable levels and fell equally dramatically; some of the capital's worst social conditions were endured and reformed, and housing passed from unregulated private landlords through state reform and later state provision. The role of the churches in providing education and welfare was overtaken by the state. The employment history of the area changed: there was huge growth in riverside industries and manufacturing and much of this work was casual and unskilled. Almost all of the inns closed or were demolished. St Thomas' Hospital left the area and Guy's expanded hugely. The road pattern of previous centuries has remained, but was supplemented by new thoroughfares. The railway cut a swathe through the middle of the town.

PEOPLE AND SOCIETY

For much of the 19th and early 20th century the Borough had a reputation for some of the very worst social conditions in London. Some of this reputation may have been based on the exaggerated prose of social reformers and journalists wishing to move or shock public and political opinion into reforming action, but it was based on more than a grain of truth. At its heart was poverty, overcrowded and poor quality housing and lack of proper sanitation.

Population

Population figures for the area this book covers are hard to establish as it cuts across parish boundaries, but taking the area as all of St Olave's and St Thomas's parishes, half of St Saviour's, a third of St George's and a quarter of Newington the population in 1801 was about 28,700; in 1821 it was 38,900; in 1851 it was 51,400, and in 1891 it was 58,700. By way of comparison the area's population today is probably a little over 20,000. Therefore, for more than 40 years, there were more than double and approaching three times the population of today, squeezed into a much smaller area, as much of the land was given over to industry, warehousing and commerce. Within this pattern over time there was a major shift in population away from the riverside parishes to developing suburbs farther south. This process was hugely accelerated by the displacement of people for the railway extension to Cannon Street and Charing Cross and for Southwark Street in the mid 1860s. In the early 20th century the population of the whole area started to decline and by 1931 was at about two thirds the 1891 figure.

The area's population growth was as a result of immigration, not of an increase in births over deaths. The vast majority of immigrants came from Britain and in particular from south and south-east England, although there were sizeable groups from Ireland (who settled in all of the poorer parts of London) and the Welsh (particularly those associated with the dairy trade).

The Charles Booth poverty map of 1889.
Note the extent of the areas coloured black, representing extreme poverty. More apparent on the original map, is the large extent of areas given over to commerce.

The Borough offered new immigrants access to work, albeit of a relatively unskilled and casual sort. In particular the railway, riverside wharves and docks, labouring and building trades offered employment. It offered accommodation of an inexpensive, casual sort, and usually of the poorest quality. The Borough also offered a society where newcomers could find anonymity and start a new life without too many questions being asked about their previous one.

The two areas with the most overcrowded and insanitary housing were in and around Tabard Street and to the west of Borough High Street both north and south of Marshalsea Road, especially near Redcross Way and Lant Street. Commentators, especially the philanthropist and social investigator Charles Booth and his surveyors, remarked on both social conditions and on standards of behaviour. While it was acknowledged that social conditions were at their worst in Tabard Street, behaviour, including endemic violence, robbery, drunkenness and prostitution was at its worst in Redcross Way. The most systematic, thorough and vibrant descriptions come from the surveys conducted by Charles Booth and published between 1889 and 1903. While the best-known publications resulting from their work are the poverty maps, the related notebooks and narrative surveys give a huge amount of information on the work done by churches, charitable and benevolent institutions.

In the 1890 survey, Redcross Way and Redcross Place were described in the following, unflattering terms: *"There is in this round a set of courts and small streets which for number, viciousness, poverty and crowding is unrivalled in anything I have hitherto seen in London... the worst specimens are found in the common lodging houses. They are prostitutes and bullies, about half the prostitutes are Irish women and their gains are made far more by robbery than by prostitution... Women decoys at entrance [to Redcross Place]... Many evil faces at windows... Rough children and lads of 14 or 15. Holey, ill clothed, dirty, well fed... 'Police don't go down here unless they have to and never singly."*

The quote is from the policeman, who accompanied George Duckworth, author of this piece and Booth's surveyor.

Poverty

A major trend of the 19th century was the increase in levels of poverty in the area. The closure of the high street inns and the move of St Thomas' Hospital with its associated professional and teaching staff removed two of the town's social elites. The increase in poverty was also accelerated by the building of the railways and trams, which enabled more prosperous folk in more regular employment to move to newly-built suburbs. The remaining population, many without full time or permanent jobs, were forced to remain close to places, such as the riverside docks, warehouses, and factories where casual work could be found. For many families women were the major earners, working in food processing factories such as Pink's jam factory or, in the late 19th and early 20th centuries, as cleaners in City offices.

The problem of poverty expressed itself in overcrowded and poor quality housing and in the high levels of sickness and disease.

The state considered it had a minimal role in providing for the poor. It continued to exercise this through parish-based poor relief, which was delivered much as it had been in previous centuries. The poor law was reformed in 1834, with further modifications in 1869. In 1834 responsibility for poor relief was taken from the parishes and given to newly-formed Poor Law Unions (i.e. unions of parishes) administered by Boards of Guardians. In 1869 the unions were further reorganised. The St Saviour's Board of Guardians administered St Saviour, St George the Martyr, St Mary Newington (and Christ Church) parishes and the St Olave Board of Guardians St Olave, St Thomas and St John Horselydown (along with Bermondsey and Rotherhithe). This reform was the first to split apart the area of the Borough and the pattern it established was later used for the boundaries of the registration districts and later again the Metropolitan Boroughs.

The regime was tightened and the availability of out relief (such as money or fuel) was greatly reduced. A workhouse was built in Newington in 1852 and this became one of the workhouses for the St Saviour's Union in 1869. The workhouse was seen by the state and by the urban poor as a place of utter last resort. Both the conditions encountered by its inmates and the social stigma associated with it ensured this pariah status. While many of the Guardians were content to run affairs to the low standard expected by central government, there were examples of social reformers being active in the working of the poor law. One such was Janet Johnson, who, in 1888, became the Southwark Board's first woman guardian and did much to improve conditions for infant children in the workhouse.

Despite the poverty of the area in the late 19th century, only 2% of the population were in receipt of assistance from the Board of Guardians: testament indeed to the independence of spirit of the residents and the stigma of an institution they shunned.

The Boards of Guardians were abolished in 1930 and their welfare and health functions were transferred to the London County Council.

Settlements and charities

Across London other bodies started to undertake religious and social work. These were missions or settlements, voluntary bodies independent of the parochial structure, but frequently with their roots in the Anglican church. Very often they were established by universities or public schools and drew their clergy and helpers from within the founding body. Charterhouse School (originally in Clerkenwell, but which moved to Godalming, Surrey in 1872) set up a settlement in Tabard Street in 1885. The school had no particular association with the Borough, but it has been suggested that it was stimulated by the appalling housing and moral conditions described by the Rev Andrew Mearns in his hugely influential pamphlet, *The bitter cry of outcast London,* published in 1883.

The mission (the person in charge was called the missioner) worked from the very heart of the poorest part of the Borough in Tabard Street and from an address Charterhouse occupied until very recently. Their four aims were to encourage local residents to attend church; to improve their behaviour; to provide them with diversions from what Charterhouse saw as the prevailing vice and temptation, and to civilise residents through visits to the countryside and especially to the school at Godalming. Initially Charterhouse had a tiny chapel in Tabard Street and after 1892 a separate one, St Hugh's, in Crosby Row nearby on the north side of Long Lane. Until the late 20th century the missioner was always an ex-member of the school, and the post was a permanent, and very demanding appointment. All his assistance was from volunteers, very frequently pupils or ex-pupils from the school. As the 20th century progressed so its work became increasingly secular and much emphasis was put on its youth work, particularly with boys.

Charterhouse was not the only settlement active in the area, as the Mint and Gospel Lighthouse Mission of the Shaftesbury Society was based in Union Street at its junction with Redcross Way. The main focus of its work was assisting girls.

Housing

Until the middle of the 19th century, virtually all residents rented their homes from private landlords. For most this was no more than rooms in a house with meagre, shared facilities and an intermittent water supply.

Most tenancies were of a casual and short-term nature. For the most part neither landlord nor tenant felt much responsibility to each other. Midnight flits to avoid the rent collector were as common as landlords neglecting to maintain their properties.

Landlords often used lettings' agents for the day-to-day administration of their properties and these agents often provided a buffer of information and scruple between landlord and tenant. In one instance the agent Clutton, working on behalf of a landlord, to whom the Ecclesiastical Commissioners (much land was still the freehold of the Anglican Church) had let properties to the west side of Borough High Street, failed to notify (and the commissioners failed to notice) that the landlord's lease had expired and the properties were under the commissioners' direct control! Nor did landlords receive much encouragement or compulsion from the vestry to improve matters, indeed many of the vestrymen were landlords or landlords' agents, and they often did all they could to frustrate the activities of reformers.

Another important feature in housing was the relationship between home and work. For many work was casual, unpredictable and with irregular hours. (It was also usually unskilled, poorly paid and dangerous.)

Tabard Street Area, c. 1890.
Illustration: Charterhouse in Southwark.

People needed to live near their places of work, they could not afford time, the rents or the transport costs necessary to live in developing distant suburbs. So, despite poor and overpriced housing conditions, tenants were fearful of eviction by landlords or, later, state intervention, as replacement housing was likely to be preceded by a period of homelessness and to be more expensive. Moreover, for those who were self-employed, such as costermongers, or those practising more anti-social trades such as fish smokers, their home and work was inextricably linked.

The complacency and negligence of private landlords and the appalling conditions in which many people lived were sensationally revealed to a wider public in a slim, but hugely influential pamphlet *The bitter cry of outcast London* published in 1883 and further reproduced in the mass circulation *Pall Mall Gazette*. It was researched by a congregational minister, the Rev Andrew Mearns but probably written by another minister, the Rev. William Carnall Preston. For the first time the exterior and interior of the poorest working class housing were described. The essay identifies the locations it describes and two of the most graphic, both in terms of housing conditions and moral behaviour of the residents, are in the Borough. One section, *Immorality*, describes the Mint, another focuses on Collier's Rents, a narrow alley off the west end of Long Lane, on the site of the southern part of the modern Tennis Street:

"There are around the Hall some 650 families, or 3250 people, living in 123 houses. The houses are largely occupied by costermongers, bird catchers, street singers, liberated convicts, thieves and prostitutes... Entering a doorway you go up six or seven steps into a long passage, so dark that you have to grope your way by the clammy dirt-encrusted wall... the walls are separated only by partitions of boards, some of which are an inch apart... In this room an old bed, on which are some evil-smelling rags, is with the exception of a broken chair, the only article of furniture. Rooms such as this are let furnished (!), at 3s 6d and 4s [20p] a week or 8d [3p] a night."

The publication had influence in many quarters. It started a process of systematic social investigation independent of government's. This was to culminate a decade later in the work done by Charles Booth in surveying and classifying every street in inner London by its relative poverty. *The bitter cry* raised consciousness among the media, among the public in general and among the Christian philanthropists in particular. The latter group, while unable to influence housing conditions, were able to provide social welfare through the numerous settlements that were founded in the poorest parts of London in the 1880s. Charterhouse in Southwark, no more than 200 metres from Collier's Rents, was established in 1885. *The bitter cry* pricked the conscience of some of the landlords and gave encouragement to the more socially aware, semi-philanthropic landlords; it gave encouragement to housing reformers like Octavia Hill, who believed that the fundamental problem was the nature of the landlord-tenant relationship, and the only way improvement could be made was to give each side rights and responsibilities. It also encouraged some of those in government, who were starting to recognise that a fundamental factor in the long-term housing improvement would have to be an increased role for the state in regulating and ultimately providing housing for the working classes.

Graphic descriptions of poor housing became a staple of journalists. Ten years later, in 1894, *The Standard* wrote of Maypole Alley and the other tenements west of Borough High Street:

"Wretched ravines of dingy structures connected with the main street by narrow and tunnel shaped entries, are permanently excluded from their supply of light and air and afford what is designated as a close refuge for the criminal and vicious. Rows of houses, generally back-to-back, harbour a population decimated by disease and producing a race of children ever more sickly and degenerate than their parents. Child life, is in fact, blighted and a plentiful crop of pauperism is provided for the future. In short, everything connected with the locality is so bad and so hopelessly insanitary as to necessitate nothing less than a clean sweep of the whole neighbourhood."

The later 19th century saw reforms in the types of properties built and in the characteristics of the landlords. But before these are discussed we must turn to the building of the Trinity Estate, a highly unusual development of high quality houses erected by a private landlord.

Trinity Estate
The Trinity Estate was a greenfield development, made by a responsible landlord, who built high quality properties. It also survives intact. The estate is in the parish of St Mary Newington but very much part of the Borough in terms of its locality.

The Trinity Estate is so called as it was, and still is, owned by Trinity House, the body that since the 16th century has been responsible for lighthouses and other aids to navigation around the English coastline and for the welfare and training of mariners. The land came to Trinity House from a bequest by Christopher Merrick in 1661. Until the early 19th century the land was used for agriculture and market gardening but building started in 1814 after Trinity Street (then called Great Suffolk Street East) was laid out. Trinity House exercised close control over the design and quality of building and while this gives the impression of a planned development in fact it was built over a 30 year period by a series of speculative builders, working under leases granted by the estate.

At its centre is Holy Trinity Church, a daughter church of St Mary, Newington, and the first new Anglican parish anywhere in north Southwark for more than a century. The church was designed by Francis Bedford, who was also responsible for St Luke's, Norwood. The new church was consecrated in 1824. It is a stern, classical design with a slender square tower above its entrance portico. The church is unusual in having a statue near its steps and more unusual that the subject – King Alfred – is secular, not sacred. The statue was erected c.1825 as a centrepiece for the square. Its origin

An aerial view of the Trinity Estate (mid left) Great Dover Street (centre, left to right), the Tabard Gardens Estate (immediately behind) and Borough High Street, (snaking left), of 1927.

has been a matter of uncertainty and dispute; once thought to have been medieval and moved from Westminster Hall, a more plausible theory is that it dates from the early 19th century and was originally destined for a building in Manchester.

The church is the centrepiece for the first pulse in the building process – that of Trinity Square itself. The square set the tone for later additions: uniform brick terraces with stucco ground floors, semi-basements and dormer windows above the roof parapet. Trinity Square was complete by 1832; Merrick Square by 1856 and the houses on Swan Street, Cole Street, Brockham Street, Harper Road and Falmouth Road were built in the intervening years. In contrast to the social character of other parts of the Borough, the Trinity Estate was a prestigious address and its houses were soon to be occupied by some of the leading names of the area, including clergy, architects and industrialists.

The Trinity Estate was the last coherent development of the 19th century. By 1800 there were only small pockets of undeveloped land. By the middle of the century all available space was occupied either by terraced housing or increasingly by industry and warehousing. An important factor in housing provision was the increasing value of land, particularly in the later part of the 19th century. This was a result of the Borough's proximity to London and the greater profit that could be obtained from land used for commerce. This had two consequences. First, it tempted landowners to sell land once used for housing to business, and the sale of land, admittedly forcibly, to the railway companies is the biggest example of this. The second was that housing providers could not afford to buy land for housing, so even when they wished to redevelop slums – and to rehouse those displaced from demolished overcrowded slums meant building on a larger area of land – they could not afford to do so.

Charles Booth's poverty surveyor expressed the relationship between rental costs and social structure thus:

"The same change is going on in Southwark that in years past took place in the City. As site values rise those who can most afford to pay for them leave i.e. the rich leave first. After them go the fairly comfortable and last of all the poor and the very poor. Hence those who can the least afford to pay high rents are the last to leave. The rich were the first of the residents to leave the City, the poor have only just left. In Southwark the rich have already left, the fairly comfortable are leaving, the poor and the very poor remain and will remain until they are evicted."

New approaches to housing:
model dwellings and new landlords

The later years of the 19th century saw three fundamental changes in housing. The first was in the type of properties being built, the second was in the characteristics of landlords and the third was tentative state intervention in poor-standard housing.

Instead of terraced housing landlords started to build tenement-type model dwellings. These offered higher densities (simply because the blocks were higher than two-storey terraces), and so the prospect of greater income and more modern facilities. Some were built by existing landlords such as Mowbray and Stanhope Buildings on Redcross Way, built by the Ecclesiastical Commissioners and managed for them by the Victoria Dwellings Association, to the west of the high street. Most were built by more socially aware landlords such as Peabody – indeed housing of this type has become universally associated with these new, more responsible landlords. Examples include Nelson Square, later Hamilton Square, between Crosby Row and Nelson Street (later Kipling Street) and now replaced by a modern block of the same name. This was built by the loftily-named Improved Dwellings for the Industrious Classes. Other examples were Douglas Flats, south of Marshalsea Road, built in 1884 by the Improved Industrial Dwellings Co and passed to the Peabody Trust in 1964.

The landlord-tenant relationship also changed through the emergence of a group of housing charities in London. Their aim was to provide affordable housing of a higher quality, often in model dwellings rather than in terraces. Paradoxically, although charities, these bodies were established on a more organised business basis than most speculative builders. Unlike the speculative builder, whose funding for his next house came from rents from the previous, their capital came from philanthropic and well-off Victorians. The process was not entirely philanthropic and investors were offered a return on their investment, usually of 5%, hence their moniker, 5% philanthropists. To guarantee a return of this sort, the managers of these so-called new model dwelling companies needed to attract good tenants, who were in steady work, who could afford to pay their rent promptly, in full and regularly, and who were sufficiently responsible to maintain the property they occupied in a good condition. Such circumstances and behaviour from tenants was far from guaranteed in an area like the Borough, more known for its poverty, overcrowding and, in places, vice and crime. Despite the high standards Peabody required from its tenants and the fact that far from all the population of poorer London could

Redcross Gardens, Stanhope and Mowbray Buildings, 1902.
From George Sims Living London.
The buildings were erected by the Ecclesiastical Commissioners to replace decrepit slums.
The gardens were put there by Octavia Hill, when she was managing the Ecclesiastical
Commissioners' property. The youngsters of one were to benefit from the other.

meet them, in 1885, just 15 years after the first Peabody housing in south London, there was a 2 year waiting list for its homes.

The circumstances of poor quality terraced housing, its gradual replacement by model dwellings (some good, some bad) and the increasing involvement of the 5% philanthropists in housing provision were features of many parts of working class London in the late 19th century. However the Borough has a unique position in housing history as it was the focus of the work of one of the great housing reformers of the 19th century, Octavia Hill.

Octavia Hill was born into a comfortable middle class family but from an early age devoted her life to helping London's poor. In the 1860s she took on the management of properties in Marylebone and her success there came to the attention of the Ecclesiastical (later Church) Commissioners, who were responsible for much property in the

Borough. In 1884 the commissioners were persuaded by Octavia Hill to let her manage their properties in the area; she took on sites as the leases to other managing agents expired. Octavia Hill was ambitious and idealistic in her approach. Her stated aim was 'to meet the claim of the working class to be provided with healthy homes in places convenient for their occupations and at reasonable cost'. She set about achieving this in two ways: firstly through the provision of good quality and well-maintained property, along with open space and community facilities and secondly through a strictly-managed relationship between landlord and tenant. She is best known for her building of cottage-type properties and the most famous are Redcross Cottages, in Redcross Way, built in 1887. These are six tiny, but individual cottages in a rustic style, fronted by an area of open space and with an adjacent communal hall. Other similar developments followed: Whitecross Cottages, Ayres Street, of 1890, and Gable Cottages on Sudrey Street. She also greatly improved the facilities in Stanhope and Mowbray Buildings on Redcross Way. While she provided her tenants with much more than other landlords, she also expected much more of them. Rents were to be paid in full and promptly, sub-letting was not allowed and she was swift to evict those who did not meet these terms or whom she judged to be undeserving. She went on to manage all the Ecclesiastical Commissioners' property in north Lambeth and in Walworth.

Octavia Hill achieved two hugely important things: she demonstrated that cottage-style housing could be provided in inner-London, and that a new landlord-tenant relationship of rights and responsibilities on both sides, could flourish. While cottage development would never provide the solution on a large scale, the new landlord-tenant relationship she pioneered became the model for housing providers and especially for local authorities thereafter.

While model dwellings and a more mutually responsible relationship between landlord and tenant undoubtedly improved things for people who were prosperous and responsible enough to benefit, the conditions in which the very poorest lived were still hugely inadequate. The very poorest quality housing was in common lodging houses: hostels in which beds were rented in crowded shared rooms on nightly terms. The Borough had a noted concentration of these especially to the west of the high street. In the years just before World War II Southwark borough as a whole had more common lodging houses than any other south London borough and the third highest of any borough in London.

The private sector's contribution to improvements in housing standards could only be partial as ultimately its aim was a commercial one and because not all landlords saw the need to make improvements. It simply could not afford to provide good quality housing for the very poorest people, as this would inevitably require some sort of subsidy. It was not until the state became involved in housing that large-scale improvements began to take place.

Council housing

It was not until the final quarter of the 19th century that the state obtained any significant powers in housing. Until that time public bodies were limited to inspecting housing, occasionally ordering the demolition of sub-standard housing and approving proposals by the private sector for its replacement. Thus in 1877, the Metropolitan Board of Works (the London-wide administration, founded in 1856, and the precursor to the London County Council) oversaw demolition schemes in Mint Street and Webber Row, and in 1884 the authorities bought an area near Tabard Street, oversaw its demolition and sold it to a builder, Mr Goodwin, to house 280 people. Not all schemes provided enough new housing for those displaced by demolition. The demolition in 1895 of Falcon Court, the area west of Borough High Street, south of Union Street and east of Redcross Way, displaced over 800 people, but there was only capacity for 500 in new developments nearby. Nor was action always prompt. Reports of poor housing conditions in Snowsfields were first made in 1875 but it was not until after 1894 that any action was taken. The final scheme, built by the Guinness Housing Trust, only provided accommodation for a fraction of the number of the people that had been there twenty years earlier.

At the end of the 19th century local government acquired powers not just to order the demolition of sub-standard housing but to provide the replacement. Using these powers the London County Council undertook demolition and rebuilding at Tabard Street, one of the poorest and most insanitary districts in the area, with what became one of the biggest schemes in central London. Demolition started in 1910 and the first phase of building took place 1915-1925. The demolition displaced 3,500 people and the new scheme housed 2,380; the remainder were moved to Wandsworth. The scheme was a mini exercise in town planning with the laying out of new roads as well as nine blocks of flats. The Tabard Gardens development continued in later phases: two more blocks were added in the late 1920s, and nine more in 1934 after the LCC's acquisition and demolition of the nearby Pink's jam factory. While the

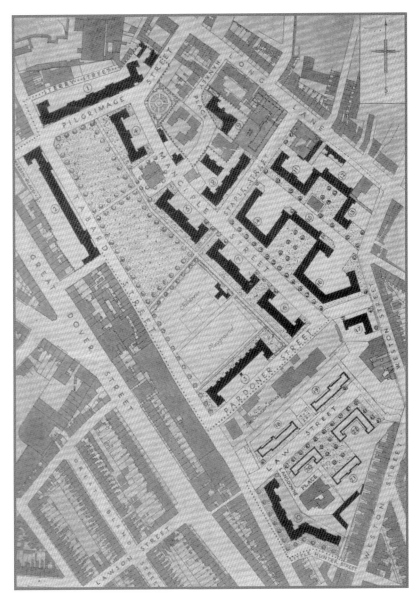

A plan of the Tabard Gardens Estate.
From London County Council, London Housing *1937 edition.*
Illustration: City of London, London Metropolitan Archives.

blocks may appear to us stark and austere, they provided a huge improvement in standard to the dwellings they replaced. Facilities included bathrooms, running water and proper heating.

While the LCC showed admirable vigour and initiative in housing matters, Southwark Borough Council (established in 1900 by the amalgamation of the parochial administrations), which also had powers to do the same if it so chose, was considerably less active – indeed it was responsible for no significant schemes in the area until after World War II. This poor record compares unfavourably with that of the radical and energetic Bermondsey Borough Council immediately to Southwark's east.

By the late 1930s there were still pockets of extreme poverty in the Borough, nearly a quarter of people were in overcrowded conditions, and the Borough was still one of the poorest parts of London. Cecil Chesterton, an investigative journalist, came to live in the Borough at this time. His description could easily have applied to circumstances a century earlier. In an unedifying comparison with other places where he had lived, he says: "*Slums have each their own individual scent... in north Southwark they are impregnated with a corpse-like aroma, the accumulation of decades of stifled human growth.*" He also describes the situation in one of the tenement blocks, which frustratingly he does not identify. Features include broken floor boards, free-running rats, no arrangements for refuse disposal and a threatening landlord. Despite these circumstances, the average standard of housing had increased massively in fifty years. A major contribution to this was the role of the state in regulating and clearing sub-standard housing and in later providing their own housing. Equally important were changes in employment and transport that allowed people to move away from the area to new estates built by the LCC, such as at Becontree, Downham or St Helier, or to the new swathes of private housing in the outer suburbs such as Welling.

Public health
The Victorian city was a very unhealthy place to live and the Borough was among its most insanitary examples. Adult death rates, infant mortality and infant life expectancy were all among the poorest in London. In the St Saviour's district in the 1860s, 50% of children did not reach the age of 5 and this figure was still at 20% in the 1890s. Prevalent diseases were cholera (there were outbreaks in 1849 and 1853), smallpox, typhus, measles, influenza and tuberculosis. In St George's, in 1857, the number of people to the acre was 184, when the London average was 30;

in the 1880s the death rate per 1000 people was 25, rising to over 30 in 1899, while, at the same time, the London average was 20 per 1000. These figures come from the annual reports on public health presented to the vestries by their medical officers of health.

The reaction of the early Victorians was to not get involved with public health matters. Nationally or locally there was neither the resources nor the understanding to tackle the problem. Locally, this attitude started to change after 1856 when the vestries were required to appoint and receive annual reports from a medical officer of health. While many vestrymen would have preferred to remain ignorant of the matters reported, the circumstances were presented in great detail and, in the case of St George the Martyr, with considerable criticism of the vestry's lack of action. St George's first medical officer of health was Dr William Rendle (also an important writer on Southwark's history). In frustration at his employer's complacency he resigned his position and sought and was successfully elected to a place on the vestry. Rendle's successor was equally forward-thinking, even-handed, uncompromising and independent in his views. He was heavily critical of both the government and of the local population. He criticised residents for not taking advantage of smallpox vaccines (smallpox was still a persistent killer of people through the late 19th century); he also discussed the relationship between disease, crime and drink and made early, but unsuccessful, calls for the provision of a municipal baths.

The causes of poor public heath conditions included overcrowded housing; chronic disease; a lack of access to health care; poor understanding of the cause, prevention or treatment of disease; an irregular and chronically polluted water supply; ignorance, neglect and drink; poor hygiene; lack of washing facilities and inadequate disposal of sewage. A polluted water supply was the cause or contributory factor in many diseases. Until the mid 19th century raw sewage was released into the Thames, which in turn was the source of drinking water. The relationship between polluted water and cholera was not understood until the 1840s and not fully broken until 20 years later. In 1855 the source of the area's drinking water was moved upstream and after 1856 the Metropolitan Board of Works built London's main sewer system. Deaths from smallpox dropped significantly in the mid-19th century after the introduction of vaccination. Typhus was spread by lice, and deaths dropped through a combination of the gradual introduction of clean and regular water, public health education, school nurses and better washing facilities – the baths on Lavington Street, Bankside, opened in 1893.

Tuberculosis was a major killer until the early 20th century. Crucial in its elimination were the public health departments of the Borough Councils of both Southwark and Bermondsey.

Schools and education

Before the introduction of state education in the later 19th century, education was not available to everybody and was provided by a large range of bodies. Church schools dominated the picture. The National School Society oversaw Anglican schools and the British and Foreign School Society Nonconformist ones. Separate from these were the independent ancient grammar schools, including St Saviour's. Education was also provided at home (for the wealthy) or through charity or ragged schools for the poorest. In the middle of the 19th century, many children, especially in poor areas like the Borough, received little or no formal education.

In 1808 the Newcomen Charity, which previously paid for children to attend the parochial school, built its own school at the corner of Redcross and Union Streets and by 1864 both the boys' and girls' schools had moved to Newcomen Street. After 1870 the school recognised that it was unable to compete with universal provision made by the London School Board. It changed its purpose to training boys and girls for industry and commerce and then in 1913 it became what it described as a Domestic Economy and Trade School for Girls, i.e. providing training for work in domestic service.

It was not until 1870 that the state became directly involved in education. The 1870 Education Act set up school boards with a duty to provide for those with no access to a school. The initiative was not welcomed by the two church-based societies, which claimed their role would be greatly diminished, if not eclipsed altogether and because the state approach was determinedly secular. London had one school board, and it rapidly set about providing schools in the areas of greatest need. Typically its buildings were much larger than earlier schools – in scale if not in architectural detail, they could easily be confused with warehouses. The London School Board set up three schools in or near the Borough: Snowsfields, strictly Bermondsey, though it took many of its pupils from the Tabard Street area and later the Tabard Gardens Estate, Lant Street School (now Charles Dickens School) built in 1877 and enlarged in 1901, and Harper Street near the New Kent Road. Snowsfields School provided 1006 places, Lant Street 1214 and Harper

Street 1002. However in the early days the availability of places did not guarantee attendance. It was not until 1876 that attendance was made compulsory, and, more importantly in a poor area like the Borough, 1891 that schooling was free.

One of Charles Dickens School's old boys was Harry Cole (1930 - 2008), policeman, resident of Queen's Buildings, and best selling author of light-hearted reminiscences of his youth and work locally. His time at the school is commemorated by a plaque on the building.

In the Borough church schools continued to thrive and St Saviour's parochial school moved to a new building in Union Street in 1908.

Secondary schooling was a rarity in the early 20th century. The only provision was at the ancient grammar schools that evolved from the St Olave's and St Saviour's foundations and the Borough Polytechnic Day School or Notre Dame School to the west. St Olave's School is discussed in *The Story of Bermondsey*. St Saviour's School suffered a decline in the 19th century and falling academic standards and numbers forced it to move to alternative, and smaller, premises in Sumner Street in 1839. However, in 1899 St Saviour's school, St Olave's school and the St Thomas' charity school amalgamated in a unified scheme of management and this laid the foundations for the modern St Olave's Boys' School and St Saviour's Girls' School. The new St Olave's Boys' School building was on Tooley Street. The new St Saviour's Girls' School, which was erected in 1903, was at the south end of Great Dover Street. The school thrived and expanded under this new scheme and through the energetic and independent leadership of Miss M G Frodsham, St Saviour's first headmistress. Pupil numbers expanded from 388 in 1913 to 545 in 1923 and a new wing was added in 1928.

LOCAL GOVERNMENT

The Borough's complicated, conflicting and multi-layered government of previous centuries continued into the 19th century. The parish, the county, London-wide bodies, the City of London, and Parliament all had a role.

In the 19th century the arrangements for governing London were complicated, but even by the standards of the day the arrangements in the Borough were particularly confusing. The typical pattern outside the City of London was for local administration to be dealt with through parish level administration, properly called the vestry, while the county, through the court of quarter sessions overseen by magistrates, oversaw the vestry's activities and dealt with wider matters. What we would think of as capital projects, such as the building of roads, were authorised by local Acts of Parliament.

Parish administration was exercised through the vestries of St George the Martyr, St Mary, Newington, St Thomas, and St Olave and its equivalent, the grandly-named Corporation of Wardens of St Saviour. Across the whole of London, this local tier of government was reformed in 1856. Some vestries kept their name, but were given new constitutional arrangements and powers, such as with St George the Martyr, and some were superseded by Boards of Works. The St Saviour's and St Olave's boards of works date from this time. The 19th century also saw the establishment of additional local boards and commissions set up for specific purposes.

As part of a further London-wide reform in 1900 the boards of works, the vestries and other local boards and commissions were abolished and their functions were taken over by the newly-formed Metropolitan Boroughs. The areas administered by St George the Martyr, St Mary, Newington and St Saviour (along with Christ Church on Bankside) became part of the Metropolitan Borough of Southwark and the area administered by the St Olave's Board of Works (along with Bermondsey and Rotherhithe) constituted the Metropolitan Borough of Bermondsey. While this greatly simplified the way the area was administered it also split the ancient town of Southwark and the Borough into two separate administrations of very different character. This split remained until the formation of the London Borough of Southwark in 1965.

In 1856 a new body with London-wide responsibilities was created. This was the Metropolitan Board of Works (MBW), which had responsibility for building London's main sewer system and for main roads. It was superseded in 1889 by the London County Council (LCC) and at that time the County of Surrey's role in the administration of the Borough ended. The London School Board's functions passed to the LCC in 1904.

In the Borough the pattern of parish and county administration was additionally complicated by a number of factors. The first was the City of London, which owned much of the land and had powers to deal with minor criminal and civil legal cases, as well as more general administration. The City's commitment to its administrative duties was

St Saviour's War Memorial, Borough High Street, 1922.

far from diligent and the trend over the 19th century was for its influence to wane. One of the key factors for this was that the cost of proper and effective administration would have been far greater than the revenue Southwark could have provided, and the City did not want its poor and semi-detached district to be a drain on its finances. After 1835 the City's magistrate ceased to hear cases daily and consequently the quarter sessions, which heard more serious cases referred to it from the magistrate, also declined. This decline is best illustrated through the fate of the two buildings most associated with the City's role: the town hall and the Borough Compter Prison. The site of the town hall at St Margaret's Hill was leased for other purposes from 1859 and the prison was sold in 1853.

There are two reminders of the long-standing municipal association with the site of the first town hall: the name Town Hall Chambers for the building (now a bar) and, more dignified, the town's war memorial In fact this was the third choice for a location for a memorial to the men of Southwark who lost their lives in the Great War. It was erected by the parishioners of St Saviour and handed to Southwark Borough at its unveiling in November 1922.

The second complicating factor in local administration was the numerous boards of commissioners established for particular purposes. Examples were the Great Dover Street and the Trinity Street Paving Commissioners, set up in 1830, and the Library Commissioners for the Parish of St Saviour, who established the St Saviour's Library in Southwark Bridge Road, in 1891.

The final complicating factor was that some responsibilities remained with bodies that had been superseded. Thus while the St Saviour's Board of Works took over most of the functions of its predecessor the Corporation of Wardens of St Saviour, the Corporation of Wardens retained responsibility for administering parochial charities. More significantly the courts of three manors that the City bought in 1550 continued. Although they had few and diminishing responsibilities – for example the role in preventing and investigating crime was largely superseded by the establishment in 1829 of the Metropolitan Police – the courts continued to meet and in fact assumed a new role of drawing attention to (the many) instances of poor public health and housing. The courts continue to meet to this day, though only to enjoy a formal dinner, not to transact any meaningful business – even this is a legacy of medieval administration whose survival is as extraordinary as that of the medieval fabric of the cathedral.

A final quirk of local administration was an opportunistic appeal made in 1897 by some of the Southwark parishes for them to be made a full part of the City of London. This followed an investigation into London's government (not half a decade after the establishment of the LCC, which was meant to settle the question). This proposal was supported by the City, which wished to counterbalance what it saw as the potentially overwhelming power of the LCC. The City's support came despite the fact that the previous century had seen its interest in Southwark wane dramatically. The proposal was opposed by the LCC and Southwark's neighbouring parishes and eventually lapsed. However the episode provided a useful debate on local government and contributed to the measures that in 1900 established the Metropolitan Boroughs and saw all but an end to the City's influence in the area.

CHURCHES AND RELIGIOUS LIFE

The Anglican church faced a number of challenges generated by the Borough's huge increase in population during the 19th century and the appalling social conditions in which its people lived.

The first challenge was the provision of new parish churches. The earliest – consecrated in 1824 – and most distinguished of these is Holy Trinity, on the Trinity Estate in Newington. New churches in the poorer areas were slower to follow: All Hallows', Copperfield Street (a daughter church of St Saviour) was built 1878-80; St Stephen, Manciple Street (1850); St Alphege, Lancaster Street (established 1873); St Michael and All Angels, Lant Street (1867 and enlarged 1904), daughter churches of St George the Martyr. In addition St Saviour had a mission church in Redcross Place.

All but Holy Trinity were built in areas of extreme poverty and, according to many accounts, lawlessness and low moral standards. Unsurprisingly many people viewed the church with indifference and only a minority regularly attended its services. St Alphege's and St Michael's Lant Street were the most active in trying to attract congregations, usually by offering generous welfare provision, which was dependent on attending services (an arrangement social investigator Charles Booth severely criticised). St Alphege's, in its parish reports, was the most explicit about local residents' apathy to the church's religious offerings.

In keeping with the expansion of the 19th century, St Saviour's church underwent two substantial renovations during this period. However, the first was preceded by a period of doubt and controversy. In the early

19th century the church was threatened by neglect, poor repair and calls for its demolition. This was due to the expense of its upkeep and also by the realignment of Borough High Street to the west of its ancient route as part of the approach to the new London Bridge. This brought the main road to within 20 m of the church fabric. The case to retain and enhance the church was won and in the 1830s local architect George Gwilt oversaw renovations to the east end of the building. Much larger works took place in the 1890s, this time of a different motivation: to prepare the building for its planned status as the cathedral church of the new Diocese of Southwark. The work was overseen by Sir Arthur Blomfield and saw the construction of a new nave. St Saviour's became a cathedral in 1905, the focus for the new diocese, which covers all of inner-London south of the Thames and north-east Surrey.

St George the Martyr enjoyed a more stable history for much of the 19th century. It was refurbished in 1807–8, when the need for new foundations was recognised. In 1897 a new ceiling in moulded plaster was added to designs by Basil Champneys to the words of the Te Deum: We praise thee, O God. The churchyard was enlarged in 1817, the crypt was closed for burials in 1834 and the churchyard took no more burials after 1857. The churchyard was laid out as a public garden in 1882. Those buried in the crypt were removed to Brookwood Cemetery in Surrey in 1899.

The urban surroundings of the church caused it damage in the late 19th century, partly from increased road traffic and partly the vibration from the nearby railway. By the 1930s the building was significantly out of alignment.

While the 19th century was undoubtedly a period of expansion for church building, the early 20th century saw two contrasting events in the Anglican Church's presence in the area. The first was the elevation of St Saviour's as the cathedral church and the second was the start of the contraction in the number of Anglican parishes, a process that was to accelerate hugely after World War II.

An early victim of this contraction was one of Southwark's ancient parishes, St Thomas's, which ceased as a parish in 1898, but had much of its purpose removed in 1862 when the hospital moved to Surrey Gardens in Walworth. However it gained a new function in 1905 when it and adjoining buildings became the Chapter House for the newly created Cathedral of Southwark.

A more permanent victim was St Olave's on Tooley Street. By the early 20th century Tooley Street was overwhelmingly commercial. The ancient church suffered by having almost no congregation and was eclipsed by the much larger and more financially secure St Saviour. In 1918 the

Hay's Wharf, 1925.
The energy of the wharf is diluted by the condemned St Olave's church behind.
A sketch by H Fletcher.

St Olave's church, Tooley Street, 1925.
Already dissolved as a parish and all but the tower scheduled for demolition; the last insult is that nobody appears to want to buy it.

parish was dissolved, ownership of the site was transferred to Bermondsey Borough and permission was given to demolish all the building except the tower. Demolition took place in 1926 and inevitably, and despite protest, the tower was felled two years later. The site was acquired by the Hay's Wharf Company, which built on it their new headquarters, St Olaf House. The tenor bell, the font and the pulpit were removed to St Olave, Mitcham and the base of the altar to St Mary Magdalene, Bermondsey.

The Anglican church did not hold a monopoly in the area. There was a flourishing non-conformist tradition. One of its principal representatives was the Pilgrim Fathers Memorial church, which was closely allied to the Congregationalists. In 1863 they moved from their building on Union Street to a new one at Buckenham Square near the junction of the New Kent Road with Great Dover Street. Like the Pilgrim Fathers, the Maze Pond

Baptists could trace their origins back to earlier centuries. They had their own chapel and burial ground at the corner of New Street and Maze Pond until 1877, when they moved to the Old Kent Road. The Brunswick Methodist Chapel stood on Great Dover Street from 1835 to 1934 when it merged with St George's Hall. There was also a Methodist Chapel on Long Lane and a Welsh Presbyterian chapel on Falmouth Road.

The Roman Catholic parish of the Most Precious Blood was built in O'Meara Street in 1892.

PUBLIC BUILDINGS:
HOSPITALS AND PRISONS

Guy's Hospital
Throughout the 19th century Guy's Hospital continued to expand hugely. Hunt's House (on the site of New Hunt's House) and named after William Hunt, a governor and benefactor, was built in two stages, in 1853 and 1871. Its site had previously been warehouses. By 1870 Guy's occupied all the land between Newcomen Street and St Thomas' Street. The ornate Victorian Romanesque Keats' House, just west of the hospital's main entrance on St Thomas' Street was built in the 1860s and has been used as private consulting rooms by hospital doctors. Student accommodation was provided after 1890 in the so-called Guy's Hospital College until its site was taken over for Guy's tower. In the inter-war years the Queen Anne style Shepherd's and Henriette Raphael houses were added across the main campus green from Hunt's House. The Nuffield Building dates from 1934 and Shepherd's House was used as the School of Nursing 1921–1994. In the early 20th century the hospital acquired property on Newcomen Street from the Newcomen charity.

St Thomas' Hospital
St Thomas' Hospital quickly capitalised on the opportunity offered by the realignment of the high street in 1830 to serve the new London Bridge. In 1833 it drew up plans for a major building campaign and two new wings adjacent to the high street were erected. The north wing, also called Guy's block, was built in 1836 and the south wing, also called the Frederick block, in 1842. After the hospital's closure, the north block was sacrificed to Denman, later London Bridge Street, while the south block still stands, occupied by the Post Office.

St Thomas' Hospital, c.1861.
*An early and last view of the hospital before its demolition. The new blocks of 1836
and 1842 flank the view, the two courts of 1693-1709 are behind. In the background
(centre) is the Railway Hotel and (left) the stations' buildings. While the only obviously
recognisable landmark is the tower of St Thomas' church, (right), in fact the right hand
of the two blocks still survives as the Post Office, though disguised by surrounding
buildings on the high street.*

While one improvement in transport provided an opportunity to expand
the hospital, a later one provided it with a reason to move. The arrival
of the railway in 1836 and the gradual growth thereafter of London
Bridge Station immediately to the north, was a great inconvenience and
a barrier to the hospital's function and any expansion. The inevitable
extension of the railway west from London Bridge was the final
provocation and the hospital secured generous terms in the Act of 1859
that gave permission for this work. The compensation it received funded
the building of a new hospital on the Lambeth riverfront, to where it
moved in 1871. In the interim it occupied the empty buildings of what
had been the Surrey Gardens Music Hall in Walworth.

One common feature of both hospitals was their role in medical education. This was formalised at St Thomas' in the early 18th century and expanded greatly at the end of that century under Sir Astley Cooper. Great emphasis was placed on anatomy and in particular classes involving human dissections. This obviously required a steady supply of good quality corpses and Cooper and his colleagues developed a morally dubious relationship with their unwholesome suppliers: the so-called resurrectionists. These were unscrupulous folk prepared to scout for, dig up and remove, without the family's permission, the recently buried and make them available to the medical schools. Cooper and his colleagues not only fuelled this trade, but provided support for the men and their families during their inevitable periods of imprisonment. At time of shortage the medical schools also used animals including, on one bizarre occasion at St Thomas', an elephant.

Guy's and St Thomas' were not the only providers of health care. Dispensaries, such as the Surrey Dispensary, founded in 1777 and situated in Trinity Street at its junction with Great Dover Street, provided medication to the poor and midwifery services. Local authorities, especially after World War I, provided clinics, and the infirmaries of the Poor Law Boards of Guardians took on the role of public hospitals. Those people living in the area covered by the Bermondsey Guardians would have been treated at St Olave's Hospital in Rotherhithe and those people in the area covered by the Southwark Board at Dulwich Hospital, which was built in 1887. These hospitals passed to the LCC in 1930.

Prisons

The Borough's prisons continued as major features until well into the 19th century. In 1799 the Surrey County Gaol moved to purpose-built premises on Newington Causeway. In 1811, the Marshalsea, by this time in an exceedingly ruinous state, moved into the building just north of St George's church vacated by the county gaol. It was here that Charles Dickens's father was imprisoned for debt in 1824 and where the young Dickens visited him. Dickens took a lodging in Lant Street, at the very heart of the most disreputable and disorderly part of the Borough during these visits. Though undoubtedly a painful experience for the young Dickens these events stimulated and were interwoven into his later fiction. In *Pickwick Papers* he describes the Mint with devastating irony:

"There is a repose about Lant Street in the Borough, which sheds a gentle melancholy about the soul... In this happy retreat are colonised a few clear-starchers, a sprinkling of journeymen bookbinders, one or two

prison agents for the Insolvent Court, several small housekeepers, who are employed in the docks, a handful of mantua makers and a seasoning of jobbing tailors. The majority of inhabitants either direct their energies to the letting of furnished apartments or devote themselves to the healthful and invigorating pursuit of mangling... The population is migratory, usually disappearing on the verge of quarter day and generally by night. His Majesty's revenues are seldom collected in this happy valley, the rents are dubious and the water communication frequently cut off."

More significantly the Marshalsea is the backdrop to his great novel of 1857, *Little Dorrit*. Not only is the prison, its regime, the legal background to imprisonment for debt and its prisoners described in great and accurate detail, but the novel spills out onto the streets of the Borough. In its most touching scene, the exhausted heroine, Amy, is locked into the vestry of St George's church and rests her head on one of the parish registers as her improvised pillow.

The Marshalsea Prison was broadly the same shape as a typical high street inn i.e. of a narrow frontage to the high street and stretching away from it with a series of buildings around a yard. In 1842 the prison was abolished and all that remains of the fabric is the impressive and foreboding wall separating the alley which gives access to the entrance to Southwark Local History Library and to the northern part of St George's churchyard.

Although the Marshalsea Prison was abolished, imprisonment for debt remained and remaining debtors were moved to the Queen's Bench prison on St George's Fields. There they remained, under a stricter regime than previously, until imprisonment for debt was abolished in 1869 and the prison closed.

By way of contrast the Surrey County Gaol was in new and purpose-built premises at Horsemonger Lane, on Newington Causeway. However its contribution to judicial history is as gruesome as the Marshalsea. Notoriously, the gaol was used for public executions. One such, in 1806, of Richard Patch, Sarah Herring and Benjamin Herring attracted a crown of thousands, indeed there were three deaths, such was the zeal to view the event. It was here in 1849 that Charles Dickens witnessed the hanging of the Mannings, and in his letter to *The Times* newspaper he expressed his dismay at the spectacle and the crowd's behaviour. This started a debate on public execution, which was finally abolished in 1868. Horsemonger Lane Gaol continued to house prisoners until 1878 and at that time the prison area was cleared and turned into a public park. The court house element of the complex has expanded with enlargements and rebuildings in 1875, 1913–1917, (when the present building was erected and when it became home to the quarter sessions court for London, which transferred from Clerkenwell), 1958 and, finally, in 1974.

The final prison to survive into the modern period was the Compter, by then on Tooley Street. It was closed in 1853 and the building demolished three years later.

Other public buildings
Farther south on the east side of the high street were two public buildings: the post office and the police station. There was a post office in Borough High Street from the early 19th century until 2008. It was on the east side and south of Great Dover Street from the late 19th century. In the early years of the 20th century the Post Office broadened its functions to become the main sorting office for the district. The first police station was built in 1844 and a new building was erected across the road in 1868. The first station gave its address as Stone's End: a reference to the end of the paved road before it gave way to the marshy track of Newington Causeway and the southernmost point of the Borough. The station could well be thought to be distant from the town centre, but it was very well placed for access to the notoriously lawless area of the Mint. The police court was conveniently nearby. The police station was rebuilt and extended in 1938. In the late 19th century Southwark's County Court was in Swan Street.

DAILY LIFE

By any measure, for many of the Borough's residents daily life was exceedingly unpleasant during this period. Poor health, overcrowded, insanitary and decrepit housing, little education, irregular, poorly paid and dangerous work and virtually no state or private welfare, were uncivilising features. Many people felt they owed little to society and not much to lose by showing scant respect for their wealthier and not-so-wealthy peers.

Anecdotal evidence, and there is plenty — Mearns's *The bitter cry*, Booth's poverty surveys and Dickens's novels — all stress the lawless nature of the area. The immediate vicinity of Mint Street had the worst reputation. Mearns recorded thieves, prostitutes, liberated convicts and brothels. The Redcross Way area was little better with Booth noticing prostitution and violence. Of Redcross Place and its notorious women's common lodging he says:

"Any man at all the worse for drink has a bad chance if he once gets in here at night; he is sure to be robbed of everything and is lucky to get out of the place without bodily injury"... *"every woman there is a prostitute"*... The Superintendent said that out of all the cases at the South London Police Court more than half came from this area. *"Last year there were over 4,000 charges from this block of streets."*

There were more than a dozen deaths a year due to violence reported in the medical officer of health reports in the 1880s. There is also an allegation that the word hooligan (first heard in 1898) originated from a particularly troublesome family surnamed Hooley, though there is no evidence for this.

While these accounts are true in general terms and do give a picture of a society considerably more lawless than the most lawless parts of Britain then or today, the absence of systematic crime statistics makes any more sophisticated conclusion impossible. However some of the more sensational statements are made without evidence and this undermines their credibility. This is most apparent in *The bitter cry* where Mearns, who describes one occasion when one of a pair of burglars murdered his companion, returned to the victim's wife, claimed that his companion had been caught and took her for his partner. Another statement claimed that the corpses of nine infants were left in an undertaker's doorway.

Low-level nuisance was also a feature of local life. The authorities of St George the Martyr complained in 1904 that there was a persistent problem of residents disposing of dead cats by throwing them over the temporary hoarding then surrounding the church while the extension of Tabard Street through its churchyard was being built.

Commentators have made similar exaggerations in their remarks on residents' morality. There are many general statements about drink, violence and vice and others about relationships and co-habiting practices outside marriage, particularly among the costermongers. Many such are given by the energetic vicar of St Alphege's parish in his annual reports of the 1890s, but he was hardly a disinterested observer. However, evidence of Mearns's sensational statement that incest was common is yet to be found.

It is reasonable to conclude that some people in the Borough lived a life that was well short of the Victorian ideal and one we would find deeply shocking when judged by our own impression of Victorian standards. What must also be considered is that social conditions and pressures in the area put the temptation of drink, crime and vice in many people's way and, given the hopeless situation many saw themselves in, succumbing to temptation was all too easy. What must also be considered is that there were many residents attempting to live a life free from crime and immorality and there were many active in the church and other bodies doing all they could to support them in this endeavour.

For most people there was little opportunity for recreation. Social contact was restricted to family, work, pub or church. However, from the later 19th century the music halls and later cinemas at the nearby Elephant and Castle, or in the west end would have provided an occasional diversion to those with sufficient time and money.

Open spaces
The Borough was one of the most densely populated areas in London, and one with a young population. Despite this it was almost completely devoid of any open space. The nearest large space was that surrounding the (private) Bethlem Hospital at St George's Circus, and in the late 19th century the nearest public parks were at Southwark Park in Rotherhithe, or Kennington. The authorities had little scope to remedy this situation, but made what they could of the meagre opportunities they had.
The London County Council created a playground from part of a slum clearance area to the west of the high street. It was named Little Dorrit playground after the heroine of the Charles Dickens novel. On the opposite side of the high street an open space was made from the detached part of the disused churchyard to St George's church, created when Tabard Street was extended in 1902. Farther south in 1878 the site of the demolished Horsemonger Lane Gaol became an open space.

ECONOMY, EMPLOYMENT AND INDUSTRY
The industries and commercial activities that took root in the early modern period: leather working, printing and bookbinding, hat making, wharves, warehousing, food processing and engineering, continued to develop in the 19th century.

Hops
One trade particularly associated with the Borough has been hops. The association developed through Southwark's role in the brewing industry and its proximity to hop growing areas. By the mid 19th century two of London's most important breweries were in the area: Barclay Perkins'

Borough High Street, 1837.
A view looking north from the junction with Great Dover Street.
St George's church (right), St Saviour's (centre back) and carts laden with enormous sacks
(properly called pockets) of hops, everywhere.

brewery at Park Street, the Black Lion at Snowsfields, and the Courage Anchor Brewery at Tower Bridge. As the country's main hop growing area was in Kent, and because hops are a bulky crop, Southwark's relatively inexpensive land provided affordable warehousing, which was also conveniently close to many of London's breweries. For much of the 19th and the early 20th centuries there was extensive warehousing on either side of the high street and on land occupied today by Guy's Hospital.

Hops were picked in the autumn, very often by Southwark residents, who travelled to Kent for this annual (working) holiday from London. The hops were then dried in oast houses and in the following spring were brought to London by road. The wagons were bulky, heavy and slow. The unit of trade was the modest sounding pocket, which weighed a hefty 1.5 ctw and was about the size of a small sofa. There were two sets of traders in the process: the hop growers were represented by the hop factors, who stored the hops in their warehouses until sold, and the brewers' interests were dealt with by the hop merchants, who stored the hops between sale and their use by the breweries. The trade took place in the spring when both sides inspected samples from each pocket.

As well as the numerous and vast warehouses concentrated on the area around Maze Pond and Guy's Hospital the high street inns also had a role both as warehousing, especially after the railway diminished their trade and as impromptu offices where trading took place.

The trading process was supported by the opening in 1867 of a Hop and Malt Exchange, built in flamboyant style, on Southwark Street. The hop exchange impresses by its bulk and its light interior; good light was an important factor in assessing the quality of hops.

In the 1930s, there were 30 hop firms trading in the area, each with its own warehouse. So dominant was the trade that the letter-based telephone code for the area was HOP, translating, as proficient mobile phone texters will recognise, into the still-used prefix 407. The trade has left

London Bridge Station and Guy's Hospital from the air, 1920.
More striking than either is the extent of the largely hop warehousing in the foreground.

a physical legacy not only in the form of the hop exchange but also in the highly decorated building front at 67 Borough High Street, headquarters of W H & H Le May. The huge warehouses (with the exception of the tastefully converted Maidstone Buildings) have all been swept away. The trade has also left a documentary legacy as some of the traders' business records are held at Southwark Local History Library.

The Southwark hop trade declined after World War II, partly as a result of extensive damage to warehouse property. The trade further declined in the 1960s with the introduction of hop pellets into the brewing process, the growth of lager at the expense of bitter beers, the closure of local breweries and, in response to imported hops from Europe, the Hop Marketing Board's move of hop warehousing nearer to hop production in Kent and Worcestershire.

Rivers and wharves

The River Thames has been an integral part of the economic life of the town of Southwark and indeed the whole of the Southwark, Bermondsey and Rotherhithe districts for many centuries. The area's wharves and docks have provided employment for thousands of residents. The industries that developed through the availability of imported goods, particularly food processing, have provided work for thousands more. The import of foodstuffs and their warehousing, distribution and manufacture is an activity that was a dominating feature of the life of Bankside, Borough and Bermondsey for centuries. While food processing was focused in Bermondsey, the most important place to which foodstuffs arrived and the hub of the trade between importer and processor were both in the Borough. The key player in importing was the Hay's Wharf Company and the goods were traded at the Home and Foreign Produce Exchange in Hibernia Chambers at the London Bridge end of Tooley Street.

The demand for these foodstuffs was driven by the inability of Britain's agriculture to produce enough food to adequately feed the country's population in general and in particular London's sizeable and increasingly discriminating consumers.

By the early 20th century the Hay's Wharf Company controlled virtually all the wharves for half a mile downstream of London Bridge. The demand for its landing space and warehousing was so great that particularly during the 19th century warehouses became taller and were built farther back from the river. They dominated the riverfront filling the space back to Tooley Street and hemming in the north side of St Saviour's church. Much of the warehousing was bonded, i.e. used for goods on which duties were to be paid. The railway arches were also used for storage of these high-value goods. The riverfront landing area was increased greatly in 1856 when the company cut an artificial wet dock at the heart of their site. This was over 100 m long, 25 m wide and deep enough to take ocean-going ships.

A measure of the importance and financial strength of the Hay's Wharf Company's activities was its recovery and rebuilding after the disastrous fire of 1861. This was inevitably called the Great Fire of Tooley Street and certainly deserved its name. The fire started on 22 June 1861 and burned for almost a month. The area between St Olave's church and the cut dock (approximately 200 m east to west) and inland from the river to Tooley St (150 m) was destroyed. The fire was able to take hold as a lack of mains water meant the fire appliances present had nothing with which to douse the flames. The fire was also fuelled by the vast amount

Hay's Wharf, 1938.

of combustible materials in the warehouses and by a gentle southerly breeze. The fire made for sensational newspaper reporting and viewing for the thousands of spectators who flocked for a grandstand view on London Bridge. As well as vast destruction to property and goods, and disruption to London's food supply, the fire also claimed lives. The most famous of these was that of James Braidwood, the superintendent of the London Fire Engine Establishment. It was his death, and more significantly his service's inability to deal with this fire, that led to the formation of the Metropolitan (later London) Fire Brigade. A small plaque at the corner of Tooley Street and Cotton's Lane marks the site.

The company imported both staple and high quality foodstuffs, such as butter, eggs and lamb from New Zealand and Australia, bacon from Denmark and in the 1860s, tea, brought in elegant, graceful and nimble clippers from China. Fresh goods imported from Australia and New Zealand meant the company and the ships that served its wharves became pioneers of refrigerated transport, importing refrigerated goods from as early as the 1880s.

Goods were unloaded from the ships, some of which were able to draw alongside the warehouses, but more frequently ships were moored mid-stream and goods were unloaded onto lighters and then craned ashore.

The docks provided a huge range of employment, from the casual labourer to the highly skilled. The most skilled were the lightermen and the stevedores. The former piloted vessels laden with goods unloaded mid-stream to the wharf and the latter were responsible for loading ships to ensure their handling would not be affected by the goods in the hold.

Not only did the company own and control the wharves and warehouses, it also had a dominant position in all significant aspects of the food importing process. It ran the biggest fleet of Thames lighters, serving not only its own wharves, but many others. It also controlled much of the subsequent road transport and in the 1920's bought and incorporated the haulage firm Pickford into its empire. More significantly, in the late 19th century, the company was able to lure the businessmen controlling the import of foodstuffs from their City offices to a new provisions exchange in its premises at Hibernia Chambers, No 2 London Bridge. The exchange moved across the road to No 1 London Bridge in 1939, into the cunningly refaced building that had previously been the offices of J & J Lonsdale. The exchange reopened in 1951 after World War II and closed at the same time as the London docks in the 1970s.

No target was too venerable or precious to the company's voracious appetite to dominate Tooley Street. Even St Olave's church, by the early 20th century one of only two of Southwark's medieval parish churches on its original site, came into its horizon. The church was by this time in a poor state of repair, surrounded by the company's warehouses and with a diminishing congregation. It was decided to close the church and the site was eventually sold to the company. In 1931 they built a new headquarters on the site. It was called St Olaf House and was designed by H S Goodhart-Rendel, with a depiction of St Olave by Eric Gill. This building greatly adds to the townscape of both Tooley Street and the riverfront and deserves to stand the test of time in the way St Olave's church did.

The Hay's Wharf Co. was also able to weather attacks made on it by, on the one hand, its workforce, and the other, by government activity. Like all the docks it was closed by the 1889 dockers' strike, but during the 1926 general strike, some of its work was done by public-spirited or strike-breaking (depending on your perspective) Oxford University undergraduates. More remarkable was that the London wharves, of which Hay's was the most important, were not included in the Port of London Authority – effectively the nationalisation of the cut docks that took place in 1909, nor in later attempts to include the wharves in this scheme.

These activities, along with the wholesale fruit and vegetable market and nearby food processors, collectively gave the area the title of London's Larder, a title the Borough Market Trustees have been glad (and justified) in reusing recently to promote the launch of the retail Borough Market.

Manufacturing
Food processing was a feature of the Bankside, Borough and Bermondsey districts. One food firm with a particular association with the Borough is the jam, pickle and confectionery manufacturer W T Pink. Pink's had premises between Long Lane and Great Dover Street on a site previously used for making ropes. Like most of the food processing trades the firm employed mainly women and, in an area where many of the men relied on the docks and on casual and irregular work, Pink's was unusual in that its women employees were the main wage earners in the family. The firm employed up to 2,000 people and remained a major feature of Long Lane until its closure and demolition in 1934.

Dewrance & Co. Founders and engineers, Great Dover Street, 1930s.

The firm was also distinctive for being one of the few businesses to have been subject to strike action among its employees. Despite the nature of employment conditions in the late 19th century: long hours, irregular, poorly paid and dangerous, militant trades unionism was a rarity at least in this part of London. One exception was the strike at Pink's in 1912. At issue were the wages paid to the staff, which were as low as 8/- per week. The strike was successful and resulted in an increase of 2/- per week on everybody's wages. While important for those involved, the action is more significant as it was an early example of an improvement in working conditions – a hugely important factor in enabling people to afford better quality housing nearby, or to move away from the area and travel to work.

Food manufacturing was not the only area that provided employment for women, as especially in the early 20th century, many women were employed as cleaners in the offices of banks, insurance houses and commodity traders in the City of London.

Engineering was another major enterprise in the Borough. The biggest firm was Dewrance on Great Dover Street. The firm was founded in 1844 by a John Dewrance, a boiler maker, who had been involved with steam locomotives from their very first days. Dewrance made valves for steam engines and the premises were divided into a bronze foundry for

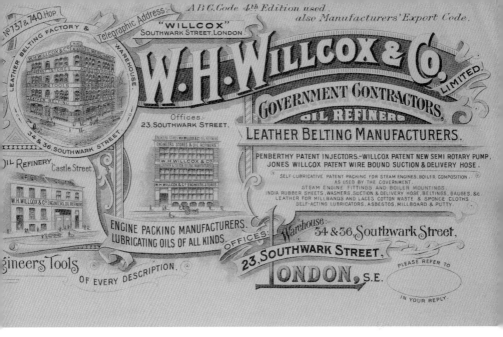

W H Willcox, letterhead of 1900.

casting the metal and machine shops for shaping it thereafter. New premises were built in 1880. In the early 20th century Dewrance employed over 1000 people. In 1938 Dewrance became part of the larger engineering firm Babcock and Wilcox. Another engineering firm was W H Willcox, engineers and oil refiners, founded in 1878, whose distinctive head office at 38, Southwark Street still stands.

Inns, market, trade and commerce
Communication and providing facilities for the movement of people and goods has always been a major feature of the Borough's economy. This continued during the 19th century. While the number of visitors to the inns fell dramatically after the coming of the railways the inns found a temporary lease of life as distribution centres for goods. Ironically they were heavily used by the railway companies, the very organisations that had put them out of business as inns. After 1874 the George was the receiving house for the Great Northern Railway and the Catherine Wheel the Midland Railway's goods' depot. This use was not to continue and in the later years of the 19th century many of the inns were demolished: the Tabard in the mid 1870s and the White Hart in 1889. The George survived and in 1937 it was given to the National Trust. Other prominent warehousing and goods businesses included the Pickford's stables and goods yard at the junction of Tabard Street and Long Lane.

Borough High Street is one of only a few high streets in the country to have almost entirely lost its retail function; even today there are refreshingly only a handful of representatives of the typical British high street. However, in the 19th century it was a thriving commercial centre. The offices of hop merchants and food wholesalers dominated its northern end, while the southern part had a greater retail presence. One of the most dominating outlets was Gainsford & Co., drapers of 161-167 Borough High Street. An unusual survival is the family firm of estate agents Field & Son, which was established in 1804. Though they no longer own the business, the family has been associated with the firm for six generations. It still trades under the family name from 54 Borough High Street.

The Borough Market supplemented the shopping experience. It had both a wholesale and a retail function and the transition from one to the other took place at 10.30 am when a bell was rung. By the end of the 19th century the retail function had died away and the market remained a wholesale one for a century. It supplied shops, restaurants and the costermongers. The costers were street traders selling from a hand pulled barrow in street markets such as East Street and The Cut. They were a distinctive and self-contained community, distinguished by their hard-living lifestyle.

The market expanded in 1839, a new glass roof was added in 1859 and a new entrance was built by 1932. The coming of the railway and in particular the extensions west from London Bridge to Cannon Street and Charing Cross were hugely disruptive to the market. The widening of the extension west from London Bridge in 1897 forced a major alteration to the market's roof. The railway was also an important means for bringing goods from producers to the market traders.

TRANSPORT

The decline of the Borough High Street inns started in the late 18th century with the building of the Thames bridges. They allowed access to London from routes other than Borough High Street and at all times of the day or night, so making overnight stops for late-night or early-morning travellers unnecessary. The importance of transport and communications in the Borough's history, once expressed through the dominance of the inns is now seen through the dominance of London Bridge Station and the great railway viaduct that carries today's trains to it.

Left: Borough High Street, 1881. Nos 146–152. A real high street of a shoe shop, rubber goods, barber and butcher. Photo by Henry Dixon for the Society for Photographing Relics of Old London.

Below: Borough High Street, c1902. A very busy scene dignified by decoration, probably for the coronation of Edward VII of August 1902. The view looks north from the main entrance to Borough Market.

Borough High Street looking south from the roof of Town Hall Chambers, 1937.

Railways

By a short margin, London Bridge was central London's first railway station. It was the terminus for the London and Greenwich Railway, also London's first passenger line. The line opened in 1836, running initially between Deptford and Spa Road, Bermondsey. The London Bridge terminus was opened in the same year and the line was extended to Greenwich in 1838. The line is built on 878 brick arches, an incongruous and hugely intrusive feature at the time of its building, as for the vast majority of its five mile length the line ran across open land. But the urbanised nature of Southwark meant that carrying the line on a viaduct caused minimal disturbance to the roads that ran beneath it. The railway's promoters also hoped to let the arch spaces for housing but this idea, along with the proposal for a tree-lined boulevard along which fee-payers could promenade along the rural sections of the line came to nothing.

While the very first station served trains of the London and Greenwich company, by 1844 the station was the terminus of the London and Croydon company, the London and Brighton Railway and the South Eastern Railway. Their varying needs, their mutual suspicion and determination to maintain independence rather than unite (a situation reminiscent of the town's complex administrative arrangements), their uncoordinated and ad hoc expansions and the effects of these on the surrounding parts of the town all characterised the railway's presence in the Borough. Above all was the fact that the railway companies' wishes virtually always prevailed over non-railway interests. The building of new tracks to London Bridge started almost immediately and at the expense of local residents, their homes, businesses and institutions. No body was sufficiently powerful to resist. St Olave's School was moved twice in two decades and St Thomas' Hospital first had to endure the railway with its associated noise and dirt as a near neighbour, before being ousted in its entirety in the 1860s.

Although the development of railways was entirely a commercial affair, permission for building lines and stations lay with Parliament and not with local bodies. Therefore each development required an Act of Parliament. A measure of the complexity and scale of the railway's construction is that by 1858 150 Acts of Parliament had been required.

The first station at London Bridge was an extremely humble affair of uncovered wooden platforms on the viaduct and approached by a slope from the high street. The second company to terminate at London Bridge was the London and Croydon, which in 1839 built a station to

London Bridge Station, c.1860.
At this time the station was only a terminus.

the north of its competitor. Shortly afterwards the London and Brighton company and the South Eastern also started using the station and the lines to it. By 1842 an additional six lines had been laid, reflecting the companies' need for independent working as well as the frequency of services. An Act of 1840 reconciled the needs of all companies and allowed for the building of the first proper station. This was complete by 1844, but typical of the frenetic pace of development, was demolished and rebuilt merely five years later. The reason for its short life was the need to accommodate the additional lines that the companies knew would have to be built to accommodate predicted demand and the removal of the goods functions to the newly-built depot at the Bricklayers' Arms near the Old Kent Road.

The new station was essentially in two parts. Perhaps it is best described as London Bridge Stations, as this separate arrangement is still very much in evidence even today. The London and Greenwich and the South Eastern (later merging and becoming the South Eastern and Chatham

Railway) companies occupied the northern part and the Croydon and Brighton companies, which in 1846 had amalgamated to form the London Brighton and South Coast Railway, occupied the southern part. The companies had their main offices to the station's western end and the shops on the sweeping curve of Railway Approach were built in 1853. The distinguishing feature of the station layout was the wall separating the two parts. This kept them entirely separate until 1928 and this wall still forms a major feature today. The London and Greenwich's original platforms are roughly on the site of the modern platforms 9 and 10.

The use of and demand for rail transport grew rapidly. In 1850 5.5 million passengers used the station; this figure doubled in four years and reached 13.5 million in 1858. New tracks followed in proportion: three in 1850 and another three in 1866, bringing the current total of eleven. All the new tracks were carried on a viaduct of the same height as the original one of 1836. While the visual intrusion and disruption during their construction was enormous, they provided (and still provide) additional and secure warehouse space. Additional lines served Croydon (opened 1846); Dartford via Woolwich - the North Kent Line (1849); Addiscombe via Lewisham and Ladywell (1858); Orpington (1865); Dartford via Sidcup (1866), and Victoria via Peckham Rye (1867). Longer distance lines spread in an arc from Brighton in the south-west to the north Kent coast in the east. Despite its combined commuter and longer-distance roles, London Bridge was principally a commuter station. One feature of an attempt to cater for longer-distance passengers was the building in 1861 of a railway hotel. This stood at the south-western corner of the complex at the junctions of Joiner Street and St Thomas' Street. It was large, luxurious and unsuccessful. It closed in 1893 and was then used as railway offices and was destroyed by enemy bombing in World War II.

The railway's expansions were made at the expense of the town and its residents. The principal institutional victims were St Olave's School which moved in 1830 and in 1849 and St Thomas' Hospital which had to endure a new noisy, dirty and predatory neighbour soon after it had undergone major rebuilding in the 1830s. The hospital proved a formidable opponent, resisting proposals for expansion to the south. However, its energy was undoubtedly sapped by the constant threat. In 1859 an Act proposed the extension of the SER west to Cannon Street and Charing Cross and the hospital opportunistically turned the situation to its advantage. New lines were built from the north of the existing station, on a higher viaduct (necessary to span Borough High Street and Southwark Street). Part of the Greenwich company's terminus was demolished to accommodate the new platforms.

The consequences for many residents was catastrophic. Many thousands of people had their homes destroyed by the building of the new lines, and no provision was made for their rehousing. The new line west formed an unholy neighbour to St Saviour's church, now closely bounded at roof level by tracks. The new line also ran directly over the Borough Market. While these bodies accepted their new neighbour, St Thomas' capitalised and although the new lines took only a small quarter of their land, the hospital ensured that the Act stipulated that if the company needed to buy any of the hospital's land, they had to buy it all. This gave the hospital its ticket to leave, and with a handsome pay off. At first they ambitiously asked for the extravagant sum of £750,000 compensation, but settled for £296,000. This covered a significant part of the costs of the building of a new hospital on the Albert Embankment and their move to it. In the early years of the 20th century the lines west from London Bridge were widened again.

Apart from the symbolic linking of the two parts of London Bridge station in 1928 (by a modest breach in the dividing wall), the major contribution of the early 20th century to rail services was in the type of traction and not in new lines or platforms. The first switch to electric power was in 1909 and lines were gradually upgraded from steam or diesel to electric, particularly in the 1920s. This provided a much greater passenger capacity and, through colour signalling, more frequent services.

By 1936 London Bridge was dealing with 2,400 trains carrying a quarter of a million passengers a day of which 80,000 travelled through to Cannon Street, Waterloo or Charing Cross. In addition the station has a long tradition of serving special events. The first was the Great Exhibition at Crystal Palace, which generated many early passengers. Later, trains served race days and families taking the annual working holiday hopping in Kent. The poorest quality rolling stock was reserved for the latter, perhaps reflecting the hoppers' low priority to the railway, or their proven poor behaviour, or the railway's prejudices.

Underground railways
Vast swathes of south London are derided for the absence of underground railways. Ironically the key technological advances in tunnelling, which made deep tube lines possible were pioneered south of the river. The first was the Brunels' Thames Tunnel between Rotherhithe and Wapping. This enterprise developed a method of

tunnelling using a shield to protect the cutting face that was both effective and safe. The second was a later use of this technology in the world's first tunnelled underground railway between the Tower of London and Vine Street, Horselydown. This was opened in 1870. While it was dependent on primitive operating systems – carriages had to be hauled by cable – and only operated for a few months, it demonstrated the potential for this form of construction. By the 1880s there was already a demand for additional passenger capacity: main lines terminated on the periphery of the City and west end and while omnibuses provided carriage, roads were chronically congested and slow. Need was further fuelled by the building of underground rail lines north of the river.

As with overground lines, all developments were dependent on private initiative and subject to Acts of Parliament for their authority. In 1884 an Act authorised the City and Southwark Subway to be built between the Monument and the Elephant and Castle. The original plan was for carriages to be hauled by cables, but the decision to upgrade the traction to electric engines made this, when it opened in 1890, the first deep underground electric railway in the country. Locally there were stations at Oval, Kennington, Elephant and Castle and Borough (opposite St George's church, and an unusual example of the area's popular name being used in an official context).

As with the overground lines, major modifications soon followed. In 1893 the line was diverted to Bank and so a new tunnel was cut north of Borough station and a new station built at London Bridge. Thirty years later, the City and South London Railway was integrated with the Hampstead line, which ran north from Camden Town. The line was named the Northern Line in 1937. To link the two lines, tunnels had to be widened to allow passage for the larger trains that used the Hampstead line. During this widening exercise in November 1923 at a point under Newington Causeway the tunnellers, working through stable London clay excavated too close to the unstable gravel above. The thin clay roof collapsed and 650 tons of gravel and water filled the void. A huge crater appeared in the road and this was followed by the collapse of a gas main and the inevitable explosion and fire. This was followed by the collapse and rupture of a water main. While the fracture of two major services would normally be a double disaster, this proved to be an unusual example of good fortune, as the escaping water put out the fire. More remarkably, no casualties were reported.

Trams

Rail travel provided quick and high capacity transport, but, ticket prices were prohibitively high for many until the introduction of workmen's fares in the 1880s. Affordable mass transport first came to Londoners with the arrival of the horse tram in the 1870s. The Borough's position in London tram history was as a destination. Tram lines, like overground railways, initially failed to penetrate the City and west end, as the authorities there were afraid that mass transport would damage the area's social prestige. Trams from south London that travelled along both the Kent Road and Great Dover Street and via the Elephant and Newington Causeway terminated at St George's church. Travellers thereafter had to walk or take an omnibus. Trams, like trains, were initially a private, commercial initiative, but a clause in the Acts that permitted them required that they be offered for sale to local authorities after 21 years. By this means many of the lines came into the hands of the London County Council.

The coming of tram and underground rail services were of indirect relevance to the residents of the Borough, most of whom would have walked to work in nearby industries. But they did have a number of important indirect consequences. The tram stimulated the building of suburbs and those among the Borough's population that could afford to move and afford the tram fare and travelling time, quitted the area. This left behind a poorer, needier population and a poorer and needier local administration. It also stimulated industrial and commercial development.

Roads

Road travellers were assisted by the building of major new thoroughfares during the 19th century. Many were associated with serving the new bridges over the Thames. However the earliest new road within the Borough was built as a by-pass. This was Great Dover Street, built 1814, as a wider alternative to the narrow Kent Street (renamed Tabard Street in 1877). As early as 1766 Thomas Smollett pointed out: "the avenue to London by way of Kent Street, which is a most disgraceful entrance to such an opulent city" and by the early 19th century Kent Street was wholly unsuited as the first stage of the main road from the south end of Borough High Street to what we know as the Old Kent Road.

There was major disruption to the northern part of the high street in the early 1830s to create a new approach to London Bridge. By the early 19th century it was apparent that old London Bridge was utterly unsuited to the demands placed on it and a replacement was commissioned. It was designed and built 1823–1831 by father and son John and Sir John Rennie. It was situated about 75 m upstream of the old Bridge and, as a consequence the high street was widened and pivoted from a point near St Thomas' Street in a slightly more westerly direction. This was to the advantage of St Thomas' Hospital, which expanded west to the new road front and the major disadvantage of St Saviour's church, which was now closely hemmed in at its east end by the new road. Duke Street was built as a new link between the west end of Tooley Street and the high street.

In 1853 some of the new capacity of the widened road was given over to a clock tower dedicated to the Duke of Wellington who had died recently. Its cost of £1500 was raised by public subscription – testament to the heroic status the Duke held in the public mind. The tower was erected in the middle of the high street, near the junction with Duke

A plan of the new approach to the south side of the new London Bridge c.1830. This plan amply illustrates the extent of the demolitions required and just how narrow the previous street was. See also inside back cover.

Street. Unsurprisingly it immediately became a major obstacle to traffic and campaigns for its removal started only five years after its erection. In 1867 it was taken down and moved to the spacious arena of the Swanage seafront. That section of the high street was also briefly renamed Wellington Street.

Southwark Street was built in 1864 and became the much-needed east-west link between the high street and Blackfriars Road (Union Street was too narrow to cope with the demand). Marshalsea Road was built in 1888 to link the west end of Great Dover Street with Southwark Bridge Road. In so doing it cut across and forced the demolition of the remaining slums of the Mint. In 1902 Tabard Street was extended to Borough High Street through part of the disused churchyard of St George's church. Shortly afterwards, Long Lane was widened at its junction with Borough High Street.

Great Dover Street was built across largely open country, but Southwark Street and Marshalsea Road required the demolition of much property and had the undesirable effect of crowding the displaced residents into an even smaller stock of housing.

The century and a half from 1800 saw huge changes in the Borough. The population grew to levels of oppressive and hugely unhealthy overcrowding and then started to fall in response to ever growing pressures on land for use as warehousing and for manufacturing. The state and private bodies became involved in providing welfare and educational services and the shape and character of the area was changed for ever by the coming of the railways.

CHAPTER 4

Recent generations

WORLD WAR II

World War II, and the reconstruction process that followed it, initiated or accelerated a number of trends that shaped the population, building and economic profile of the area for the next two generations. The first of these was a fall in population, which in 1931 stood at approximately 37,000 but by 1951 was about 20,000. The second was a vigorous programme of local authority housing and the third was the reconstruction of industry.

However, the five and a half years of wartime events that preceded these were one of day-to-day survival, destruction and disruption, rather than of planning for a brighter future. The outbreak of World War II would have come as little surprise to the residents of the Borough. Observers of the international scene would have been aware of growing tensions between Germany and the UK and observers of the local scene would have noticed the distribution of gasmasks and encouragement to build Anderson and Morrison shelters in their homes. What residents were also aware of was that their closeness to the City, to the docks and the major railways would put the area very high on the list of Germany's bombing targets.

The declaration of war triggered the long-planned evacuation of school children; a huge but needless disruption to family life. This was organised by the London County Council and was executed through its schools. Classes travelled as a unit, led by their teachers.

The reality of war on the home front got underway with the blitz of 1940 and 1941 and, after a relative lull, resumed with the VI flying bombs and the VII rockets in 1944 and 1945.

The total number of civilian war dead in the Metropolitan Boroughs of Bermondsey and Southwark together was about 1,500 and the total number of people with addresses in the Borough was approximately 150. Given the accepted ratio of deaths to serious injuries of 1:1.5 this gives about 225 people seriously injured. However the number of people killed or seriously injured in the Borough would be rather different, given its position as a place of work and through which many people travelled.

Bomb damage during World War II. Looking down Great Dover Street, from the junction with Borough High Street.
Illustration: PA Photos.

Few of the Borough's population had back gardens in which shelters could be built and so many people were forced to take refuge in other spaces that they thought afforded safety. These were either under the arches of overground railway lines or in tube tunnels. The overground railways offered much less shelter than supposed and were, of course, a target in themselves. Two incidents, which were among the deadliest in London, took place within yards of each other under the London Bridge arches. On 25 October 1940 a bomb landed on the arches in Druid Street also rupturing a gas main and killing 77 people. In fact the arch wasn't being used as a shelter, but as a games room and sports centre. On 17 February 1941 another bomb landed on the railway at Stainer Street, this time killing 57 people who were in a shelter with heavy steel doors at each end. A direct hit blew the doors in and a burst water main added to the chaos.

More effective was the shelter called 'The Deep'. This was a 600 m long disused underground railway line that ran from Borough tube station to the Thames. The tunnel was a vestige of the original City and South London Railway's course from Borough to Monument. It was converted to use as an air raid shelter by Southwark Borough Council. The shelter could accommodate 14,000 people. There were six entrances and it had bunks, lavatories and electric light. Catering was provided by the Salvation Army. Despite its size there was resentment by local people who complained about its use by people from outside the area.

As well as damage to life, World War II caused huge damage to property. Areas particularly badly hit were the streets to the north of Snowsfields; the area between the high street and Long Lane and just north of Marshalsea Road. Three VIs landed in the area: one at the junction of Swan Street and Cole Street, one between London Bridge and Hay's Wharf and one at the junction of Union Street and Great Guildford Street. The Tabard Gardens Estate and Borough Market also suffered damage. Despite being central to this destruction, and very close to the most heavily hit areas, Guy's Hospital suffered very little damage.

PEOPLE AND HOUSING

Post-war reconstruction

Those charged with the task of post-war reconstruction faced three huge challenges: rebuilding the Borough's housing, rebuilding the Borough's industry and commerce and, given the area's central role in London's food supply and transport, to do so quickly. They were led by the *County of London Plan* of May 1943 by Patrick Abercrombie and J H Forshaw. For inner south London and the east end the plan proposed a reduced population, (through the dispersal to outer areas of London) to open up the river front and to increase the amount of open space. Later London-wide plans called for an increase in office accommodation. The tension between the residents and the new commercial developments has been a constant theme for the last three generations.

Population

After World War II the population continued to fall. In 1951 it stood at about 20,000 and in 1961 was about 17,000. It was not until the 1990s that it started to grow and now stands at over 20,000. Today's population is very mixed and made up of four broad elements: a vestige of the older white working class; a younger very ethnically mixed group with families; prosperous young professionals, mainly living in the large number of new apartment schemes, and students living in the converted Dewrance building on Great Dover Street.

Housing

Despite the call for a reduced population planners could not ignore the long-standing population, many of whom wished to return to the area they considered home and where they had nearby work, especially on the river. As a consequence there was a concerted programme of building both by the London County Council, which expanded the Tabard Gardens Estate and, making a break from its pre-war policies, the Southwark Borough Council. Most accommodation was in low-rise flats and many such appeared, such as at the north end of Great Dover Street, south of Newcomen Street and on the bomb sites north of Long Lane. So swift was this building that the area was not subject to any of the grotesquely ambitious redevelopments of the 1960s and 1970s and its skyline is pierced by only one pair of high residential blocks on the Lockyer Estate.

The 1970s and 1980s were lean periods for housing in the area. Firstly, the policies of the Conservative government reduced local authorities' role and resources in housing. Secondly, while there was plenty of redevelopment in the area, it was commercial, mainly office-based, not of housing or traditional industries. Many of the new developments were opposed by a coalition of local residents represented through the North Southwark Community Development Group.

Developments of the late 1990s have certainly changed this situation, but not with housing of the type that long-standing residents would necessarily approve of. A pioneer in this field was developer Indi Johal, who, in 1998, bought and converted the long-empty Town Hall Chambers into high quality apartments; he has also carried out works of a similar character in Southwark Street. Similar, but much larger in scale, was the conversion of Maidstone Buildings, in part a 19th-century hop warehouse, just off the high street. Numerous developments followed, especially towards the south end of the high street. Unconstrained by being in conservation areas and with the availability of large plots of land that previously had a commercial use, more recent developments have not been so restrained. In particular the Berkeley Homes' Tabard Square development, which fills much of the wedge previously occupied by the Pickford's depot at the junction of Long Lane and Tabard Street is on an unprecedented scale. Although smaller than first planned, the scheme includes a 22-storey tower and 360 apartments. There has been a number of smaller developments on Lant Street.

A COMMUNITY AND ITS SERVICES

Schools
As the population fell, so did school numbers; some schools closed and others left the area. Newcomen School, which uniquely among London's schools provided 3 or 4 year courses training girls to work as hospital or nursery nurses, or in catering, closed in 1970. St George's parochial school merged with St Jude's School. The oldest surviving school in the Borough is the Cathedral School of St Saviour and St Mary Overie, which started its life in the late 17th century as St Saviour's parochial school. It is now in some of the most modern buildings in the area as it moved to purpose-built buildings off Redcross Way in 1977. Its previous building on Union Street became the office for the Southwark Diocesan Board of Education. Cathedral School's near-neighbour is St Joseph's Roman Catholic School. Its building was erected in 1966, although there has been a Catholic school of this name in the area since 1913.

A feature of post-war educational reform was the systematic and universal provision of secondary schools. The Borough today has two secondary schools: Geoffrey Chaucer City Technology College and St Saviour's Girls' School. Geoffrey Chaucer School, as it was called when founded in 1980, was an amalgamation of Paragon Boys' School in Searles Road with Trinity House Girls' School. Trinity House School had been founded in 1960 in Harper Road and the new Geoffrey Chaucer School moved into its premises. Trinity House School was notable for its new and architecturally radical premises, in particular the angular and unusual shape of the main building's concrete roof. Sadly in recent years Geoffrey Chaucer School has not achieved the standards promised by its exciting building, despite its recent rebranding as a City Technology College. It is soon to reopen as the Globe Academy.

St Saviour's on the other hand was an ancient foundation and one that, although part of the state sector, kept its distance from the education authority. It resisted post-war attempts to merge it with other schools and further extensions were made to its premises in 1964. The school celebrated its centenary in 2003; an appropriate time to observe that in the previous century it had only five head teachers.

Library

One positive outcome from the new developments of the 1970s was the provision of a long-needed public library. This was a long-overdue replacement for the old St Saviour's Library in Southwark Bridge Road, which had been closed in the early 1970s. A new library was included as a condition for planning permission in the redevelopment of a site at the south end of the high street. However, this development entailed the destruction of a late 17th-century house, possibly the gatehouse to the Marshalsea Prison. The new library was named after John Harvard. To its rear was a second reading room, storage space and meeting room. This was intended to house Sam Wanamaker's Shakespeare library, but when this idea collapsed it was used to house Southwark Local History Library, the local history and archives collection for the Southwark borough, which previously had been in cramped conditions for both storage and readers at Newington Library.

Community groups

Despite the vast improvement in social conditions after World War II and the rise of the welfare state, there still remained a need and a role for the voluntary sector in providing welfare and social services in the area. This continued through the work of the mission, later renamed settlement, Charterhouse in Southwark. In post-war years its work was increasingly secular and the provision of state welfare made many of its activities redundant. Two areas where Charterhouse did continue to contribute much to the area was through its boys' club and its work with older people, especially on the Tabard Gardens Estate, which by the 1980s had a poor reputation and was in need of refurbishment.

The North Southwark Community Development Group under the leadership of Ted Bowman took a more campaigning stance and argued against many of the more excessive commercial developments in the area. In more recent times the views of local residents have been expressed through the Bankside Residents Forum.

Churches and places of worship

After World War II St George the Martyr church was restored and in 1963 the organ underwent further renovation. The observations made by the workers in 1808 that the foundations needed attention became evident again in the late years of the 20th century when a large crack appeared between the tower and the body of the church: evidence of severe subsidence. From 2005-2007 the church was closed while new foundations and a new crypt were built.

The post-war period has seen the cathedral put itself at the heart of the area and its community. The cathedral has also expanded to its north, on to land that previously had been used for warehousing, but which before the Reformation was part of the priory. There were two building campaigns. The first was the new Chapter House, with its attractive restaurant. This was designed by Ronald Sims and opened in 1988. The Chapter House moved from St Thomas' Street. A conference centre, shop and refectory designed by Richard Griffiths opened in 2001. At the same time an area of archaeological excavation at the north-east corner of the exterior of the building was left exposed, with captions pointing out the significant features. These range from a section of Roman road to evidence of the 17th-century Delftware pottery: authentic and immediate witness of the rich and varied past.

The new Anglican churches that opened with such numbers and speed in the last half of the 19th century closed with equal speed and finality a century later. This was due to a combination of population decline and an even steeper decline in church attendance. The site of St Stephen, Manciple Street (closed 1962) is now part of the Tabard Estate; St Michael's Lant Street became the New Life Gospel Church before it too was pulled down and replaced by flats. All Hallows, Copperfield Street (closed 1971) was reabsorbed into St George the Martyr. St Alphege's Victorian church was demolished and the congregation went to worship instead in their hall. By far the most noteworthy changed use was to Holy Trinity, which was converted into one of London's premier recording studios.

One major victim of wartime bombing was the Pilgrim Fathers' memorial church on the New Kent Road. It was all but destroyed in 1941 and moved to temporary premises in a private house at 76 Great Dover Street. This too was bombed in 1944 and it was not until 1956 that a new church was built, also on Great Dover Street.

The South East London Baitul Aziz Masjid mosque on Harper Road was established in 1985. It has a congregation of approaching 800, drawn largely from the Bangladeshi community.

The area's African communities have established places of worship, such as the Christ the Resurrection church, which meets in St George the Martyr and the Brotherhood of the Cross and Star in what was the Welsh chapel in Falmouth Road.

Tabard Square 2008.
This is the largest of the housing redevelopments in the area. The thorough archaeology
before construction uncovered both the Londoners' stone and a tin of Roman face cream.
Illustration: Alan J Robertson.

Open spaces

The area's open spaces, although small, are cherished locally. Many have recently come under the management of the Bankside Open Spaces Trust. Mint Street park, St George's Churchyard and more recently Redcross Gardens have all been refurbished.

INDUSTRY, BUSINESS AND COMMERCE

Post-war revival and decline

The post-war years have seen huge changes in the physical, economic and demographic landscape of the Borough. The thrust of immediate post-war reconstruction was the re-establishment of traditional industry. This process was undeniably successful although shortlived. On the river the Hay's Wharf Company not only recovered but surpassed pre-war levels of activity. (In 1960 the total tonnage of goods imported by the Port of London as a whole was more than double that of 1935.)

These revival trends were shortlived. The 1960s and later were characterised by a steep decline of traditional industry, especially wharf activity and a rapid decrease in population and the closure of shops, schools and other services supporting residents. Set against, and accelerating these trends, was a marked increase in office accommodation.

The decline and closure of the riverside wharves had many causes, including the increased size of ships bringing imports and the process of containerisation; the fact that central- and inner-London was increasingly congested and so no longer a suitable point to start the distribution of goods around the country, and the dockers themselves, whose arcane and self-serving working systems meant that employers found it almost impossible to increase productivity or change working practices. As a result, by 1970, most Thames docks and wharves had closed. This included those between the Cannon Street railway bridge and Tower Bridge, the vast majority of which were owned and run by the Hay's Wharf Company.

Other manufacturing businesses closed, such as Nettlefold and Moser, ironmongers and steel stockholders of 170-194 Borough High Street and Dewrance & Co, engineers on Great Dover Street, who sold the site in 1989. They closed for much the same reasons as the wharves: the difficulty of transport, the constraints of working from outdated premises and increasingly high business rates.

Offices

Set against this was the unstoppable rise of the City of London as a financial centre, its insatiable need for office space and the fact that commercial rents in Southwark were a fraction of those in the City. This process was also hastened by changes in government policy. In particular, the Greater London Council's (GLC) 1970 *Greater London Development Plan* and the 1973 *South Thamesside Plan* zoned Borough as an area for office development.

The 1970s saw a gradual growth in office space, sometimes in converted buildings such as at Dombey House, at the corner of Borough High Street and Union Street of 1975, but more often in purpose-built developments, such as at 211, Borough High Street. Another developer was the City of London itself, which still owned land in Southwark, and which built a new office development at what was previously warehousing at the foot of London Bridge. The development included walkways and shops that connected with London Bridge Station. It was called Colechurch House after Peter de Colechurch, the builder of the medieval London Bridge.

This period also saw a new architectural style: high buildings. Three examples were built in close succession and proximity: Southwark Towers, on top of London Bridge Station; New London Bridge House adjacent, and Guy's Hospital Tower. The first two had no character save their bulk (Southwark Towers was demolished 2008-9), but Guy's Tower, with its distinctive anvil-headed top, is a major landmark.

The site on the east side of Borough High Street south of the junction with Great Dover Street was redeveloped in the early 1980s. At this time the building of Nettlefold and Moser, ironmongers, diagonally opposite was demolished and a new office block, Brandon House, was built.

Riverfront developments

The biggest prize for the developer was not on the high street but the riverfront. It was a prize of international significance as the closure of the wharves laid open one of the largest and most desirable redevelopment sites in London for many generations. The area in question ran from Cannon Street railway bridge to Tower Bridge and inland as far south as Tooley Street.

Its development took far longer and cost far more than ever envisaged, involved a planning process of very dubious accountability, frequently incurred the opposition of local people, Southwark Council and the Greater London Council, involved international developers that had previously never set foot in the area, radically and immediately changed the employment and architectural landscape of the area and undoubtedly made those involved prosperous beyond their wildest ambitions.

By 1971 the wharves had closed and the Hay's Wharf Company, under Sir David Burnett, obviously aware of the site's post-wharf potential, was poised as the biggest landowner in the area. With partner Renslade Investments, they put forward plans for redeveloping four riverside sectors, principally as offices. The first was the riverside area west of the bridge; then the riverside to the east; then (the largest site), the riverfront west of Tower Bridge and finally a site inland between Southwark Street and the cathedral. Hay's Wharf completed only the first of these, at Hibernia Wharf. In the early 1970s (and after much reduction to the original plan) the ugly Minerva House was built and a refurbished warehouse was let and shared between the Worshipful Companies of Glaziers, of Scientific Instrument Makers and of Launderers, as their headquarters.

London Bridge City

The Hay's Wharf Company's plans for an overwhelmingly office-based scheme for their next phase, the site to the east of London Bridge, were controversial and criticised locally. The plans were disliked by both the GLC and Southwark Council for their lack of housing provision. Plans stalled during the 1970s and it was not until the early 1980s that there was any movement. The most significant was the purchase in July 1980 of the whole site by the St Martin's Property Corporation, the overseas investment arm of the Kuwaiti government. Within months a scheme, again of offices, and designed by Michael Twigg, Brown was proposed. This failed to get planning permission and the proposal stagnated into a public enquiry.

In 1981 the site became part of the London Docklands Development Corporation (LDDC), and responsibility for planning was transferred from Southwark Council and the GLC to this unelected body. Even the LDDC lacked the confidence to deal with St Martin's new proposals and in March 1983 the LDDC proposed that the planning decision for the site be taken by central government in the form of the Secretary of State for the Environment, Patrick Jenkin. In October 1983 St Martin's proposals were approved. This high-handed and secretive decision was taken without consulting local residents, businesses, Southwark Council or the GLC and without the proposals ever being made public. It is a measure of the importance of the site that it was felt that such an key decision needed to be taken at such a high level, but it was also a measure of the contempt central government had for local government and local residents. Jenkin was crushingly criticised by both the GLC, which described the process as 'jackboot planning', and in the building and planning professional media, which called his decision 'one of the most disgraceful decisions to come out of the Department of the Environment'. The plans themselves were not made public for another three months and they too received harsh words; the *Architects Journal* described the scheme as 'architecturally nondescript as its use is socially questionable'.

The scheme, which became known as London Bridge City, (City was hardly an appropriate term for such a one-dimensional scheme) was built in two phases and cost £250m. It was overwhelmingly office-based.

The development had three main components: No1 London Bridge, in pink granite with a huge corner pillar supporting a roof over a vast void designed by John Bonnington and to be occupied by accountancy firm Price Waterhouse Coopers; Cotton's Wharf, a U shaped design of offices with associated leisure facilities by MTB architects, and Hay's Galleria, by Michael Twigg, Brown. The latter was the only one to show any imagination and to include space for public use. It built a huge glass dome over Hay's Wharf's artificial dock, which was drained and covered over. The void beneath was, predictably, converted into an underground car park. Surrounding the dock were shops aimed firmly at the office and visitor market. Amongst these monoliths is a smaller development, the private London Bridge Hospital. This is in premises converted from Chamberlain's Wharf on the riverfront and Denmark and Colonial Houses on Tooley Street. The one welcome novelty of the scheme was the opening up of a riverside walkway downstream of London Bridge.

More London Bridge
The development of the much larger site immediately downstream was an even more protracted affair. Perhaps mindful of the reception the planning process and architectural achievements had received, St Martin's published and consulted on not one, but three alternative

schemes. They were all overwhelmingly and inappropriately office-based. These were subject to a public enquiry in 1988 and two years later a pseudo-Venetian scheme was approved. The plan was abandoned, perhaps as a result of the major hiatus in the London office market in the early 1990s. A new scheme by Chapman Taylor emerged in 1996, but it too was later abandoned. The empty site was something of an embarrassment and a number of suggestions were made for it, including as a temporary home for the Royal Opera House during its refurbishment in the late 1990s.

The site was finally developed in the early years of the new millennium and was initially badged More London Bridge, later truncated to More London. It is office-based, with facilities in the form of shops for office workers and a hotel. The hotel dominates the view of the site from London Bridge Station and from Tooley Street. Unfortunately it is drab,

More London, 2008.
Illustration: Alan J Robertson.

characterless and boxy. By contrast, the office buildings are angular, bright, with a preponderance of harsh, hard, steel and glass surfaces and a tendency to capture and funnel cold winds from the winter Thames. The increased number of workers gives Tooley Street a buzz and bustle that now easily rivals the west end.

Other employers

It would be careless to give the impression that the businesses that have based themselves in the area over the last generation are all large scale and working in financial services. There is a delightful eclecticism in the range of activities, sectors and institutions to be found. Perhaps the least expected is to be found in a most successful conversion of a redundant church. By the 1960s Holy Trinity church, Trinity Church Square, Newington, the striking austere classical building by Francis Bedford of the 1820s, was no longer viable as a parish. In 1971 it was identified as a possible venue for a rehearsal hall for the London Symphony and London Philharmonic orchestras. Its location, excellent acoustic, architectural splendour and isolation from traffic and tube train noise counted overwhelmingly in its favour and two years later the church changed hands back to the Trinity Estate who then leased it to the specially-formed Southwark Rehearsal Hall Ltd. The conversion was severely hampered by a fire that almost completely destroyed the building and by the grisly discovery of 500 coffins in the crypt. Despite these setbacks the hall opened in 1974. It was named the Henry Wood Hall after receiving financial support from the fund of that name. As well as rehearsal space for the musicians it is used for recordings and very many of the great names of classical music have performed there.

The voluntary sector is well represented in streets away from the glamour of the high street. Until it moved very recently, Charterhouse in Southwark and the housing body Carr-Gomm were almost neighbours in Tabard Street. Carr-Gomm is a social landlord with a national role, and this is one of its London offices. The organisation was established through the work and benefaction of a Rotherhithe family. Also in Tabard Street is the human rights organisation Liberty.

A recent trend has been the growth of further educational establishments. Some are private, such as the London Institute of Technology and Research, and others professional, such as the British School of Osteopathy, the British Association of Occupational Therapists and the College of Occupational Therapists. There are also central government bodies, such as the National Probation Service in Mitre House. Farther south, the sorting office element of the post office was moved to Willow Walk in Bermondsey in the 1990s and the post office itself closed in 2008. The police station was enlarged in 1983.

Borough Market

The biggest single commercial transformation of the last decade has been at Borough Market. It has developed into a thriving retail market of independent high quality butchers, bakers, fishmongers, confectioners, cheesemongers, wine and beer merchants and greengrocers. This has been a huge commercial, popular and gastronomical success.

After the war the market continued its traditional role as one of London's three wholesale fruit and vegetable markets. However, its fortunes slipped in the 1970s. This was caused by the relocation and expansion of Covent Garden wholesale market to Nine Elms, Wandsworth; the increasing role and power of supermarkets with their own procurement and distribution; the unsuitability of a market site in central London from which to gather and distribute foodstuffs to outer London, and the declining population of inner-London. Despite this reduction the wholesale market still carries on, with a typical working day of 2 – 9 am: the bustle over, detritus cleared and permanent pitches locked before office workers reach their desks. Wholesale traders now mainly supply central London's hotel and restaurant sector.

In the late-1990s there started a small, occasional retail market of stallholders selling high quality, regional foodstuffs. An important early arrival was Neal's Yard Dairy, selling high quality cheeses, which came in January 1997. In 1998 a food fair was held and the public interest gave the market trustees the confidence to start a retail market. A number of the stallholders travelled considerable distances. The market took on the mantle 'London's Larder', one previously worn proudly by the food importers of Tooley Street, and grew rapidly in reputation, size and frequency. It is now the major feature on the London food scene. There is a huge range of produce on sale: fish, seafood, game, rare-breed meats, organic vegetables, dairy produce, unusual wines and speciality beers, quality bread and confectionery from over 70 stalls.

Borough Market, 2008.
Illustration: Alan J Robertson.

The fabric of the market has been undergoing gradual refurbishment over the last decade and one of the most striking additions has been the erection of the cast iron portico that was once part of the floral hall at Covent Garden.

Around the market has grown a cluster of high quality shops, cafes and restaurants. The original café was the Borough Café on Park Street, run for 40 years by Maria Moruzzi. This was a traditional greasy spoon serving the market traders. It found favour with gastronomes in search of authentic south London fare, executed with Italian style. Although it closed in 2002 its successor carries on as a market stall. The first major restaurant opening was Fish! right in the middle of the market. Its slightly prefabricated largely glass building allows diners to view the action outside and pedestrians to view the contents of their plates. It also makes pedestrians all too aware of the back-office aspects of restaurants: extractors and refuse. It has been followed by many others, some chains, others independent, all upmarket, some exclusive and some very expensive.

Traditional drinkers have been provided for by the Market Porter and the Wheatsheaf, which have prospered from the market's fame. The most historic pub is undoubtedly the George, but the nearby King's Arms has the distinction of displaying a royal coat of arms retrieved from Old London Bridge. Away from the bustle of the high street, the Royal Oak pub on the corner of Tabard Street and Nebraska Street was a struggling local. In the late 1990s it was revitalised by a determined visionary and faithful new landlord, Frank Taylor. It was refurbished, supplied with Harvey's Sussex beers and has become one of the foremost real ale pubs in London.

Shops

With the decline of the residential population has been the closure of shops. As recently as the mid 1990s there was an independent butcher and greengrocer in Newcomen Street. The recent population upswing has stimulated new openings, but, predictably, these are representatives of national supermarket chains. There are a number of specialist retailers including rivals Evan's Cycles and London Bridge Cycles on Tooley Street and the Waterloo Wine Company on Lant Street.

Tourism

The most significant change in character of the last two decades has been the opening up of north Southwark as a tourist destination. This has partly been a response to the inexorable growth of tourism and London as a world destination and because the area has a concentration of sites of genuine interest. Catalysts for the development of tourism locally were the opening up of the river walkway as part of the London Bridge City development; the irresistible draw of Tower Bridge for tour buses (and their need to recross the river via Tooley Street and London Bridge); the opening of the Jubilee Line extension, allowing fast and comfortable access from the west end, and the eventual, if initially reluctant, embracing by Southwark council of tourism as a legitimate economic activity. Tourism in the Borough has also been assisted by the opening of Shakespeare's Globe Theatre and the spectacularly successful Tate Modern on Bankside.

The first attraction in the Borough was the mooring of HMS Belfast off Hay's Wharf in 1971. The ship was built, appropriately in Belfast, and launched in 1938. She played a role in World War II in escorting Arctic convoys and was heavily involved in the Battle of the North Cape and the D-Day landings of June 1944. She was decommissioned in 1963 and, after a campaign led by her last captain, was saved from the breaker's yard, moored in the Upper Pool and opened to the public. She is now owned and managed by the Imperial War Museum.

In 1999 Southwark Council opened a tourist information centre adjacent to London Bridge. This was significant in that it was a tangible recognition by the council that the area was a major tourist attraction and the council had a role in nurturing and supporting facilities for visitors. The council was supported in this view by colleagues in the Cross River Partnership – an alliance of mainly public bodies with the aim of encouraging an even spread of development across central London. As part of the tourist information centre development Eric Parry architects landscaped the area at the foot of the bridge and erected a 15m high off-vertical white limestone needle as a landmark entrance to Southwark. Ironically, the opening of the Millennium Bridge reduced the number of visitors arriving via London Bridge; the New York bombings in 2001 further reduced visitor numbers and the centre became commercially unviable and closed. The independent Southwark Heritage Association, which in the late 1980s and the early 1990s had lobbied the council to give tourism a higher profile, continued to run their own centre in the basement of Hay's Galleria until 2003.

Southwark Cathedral has also gently repositioned itself as a tourist destination. The new Chapter House development contains a café and more recently a shop was added.

Other attractions include the London Dungeon, the Old Operating Theatre, and the Britain at War experience. The London Dungeon is a sensational and darkly humorous depiction of imprisonment, torture, death and misfortune, loosely based on historical fact. It is also a huge commercial and popular success, evidenced by its queues and the fact it is now one of an international network of similar shows. It also provides for the unusual spectacle of in-costume and made-up jailers and their victims lunching in nearby sandwich bars. The Britain at War Experience recreates the London Blitz of World War II, though there is a poignancy, and perhaps even insensitivity, that it is immediately adjacent to the sites of two of the single biggest losses of civilian life during World War II.

The Old Operating Theatre in St Thomas' church on St Thomas's Street is both the most authentic and the most educational of the commercial attractions. In the tower of the church is a 19th-century operating theatre along with surgical implements. It was used for operations until 1862 when the building, still also in use for worship, was part of St Thomas' Hospital. The operating theatre remained locked away for over a century and was discovered in 1956 and after some reconstruction was opened to the public.

The Borough's unique atmosphere has become reason alone to visit. This character of gloomy, close and grubby London has been one film makers have been keen to exploit. The market area, and the curved front of the Globe pub in particular, have been most popular in this respect appearing in films as diverse as *Lock stock and two smoking barrels* and *Bridget Jones' Diary*.

GOVERNMENT, JUSTICE AND HOSPITALS

Guy's Hospital

The post-war history of Guy's has been one of expansion, expansion and continual reorganisation. In 1948 Guy's became part of the newly-formed National Health Service. In 1993 Guy's and St Thomas' were reunited as the Guy's and St Thomas' NHS Trust.

The hospital provides general and specialist medicine to a huge catchment area of south London and beyond. Its regional rather than local nature was brought sharply into focus by the strongly-opposed closure of its Accident and Emergency department in the mid 1990s. Indeed, for a while there was a threat to the whole hospital.

There have been a number of major post-war additions to the buildings within Guy's Hospital. This has largely been at the expense of ex-warehousing to the east of the original site. More recently there have been developments to the west, where new build has nibbled so far into the back of many of the inn yards that it almost breaks through onto the high street. The first development was the 11-storey surgical block, New Guy's House. This was started in 1957 and completed in 1961. The second is the dramatic and dominant 30-storey Guy's Tower of 1963-75. This contains maternity and clinical wards and the school of dentistry at its top. Wolfson House, a hall of residence for medical students was built in 1977 and the Greenwood Theatre, at the corner of Snowsfields, was built in 1975. The most recent major work is new Hunt's House of the late 1990s.

In addition to the large-scale developments there has also been a number of smaller additions that have greatly added to Guy's environment and heritage. In 1992 a peace garden between Hunt's House and Shepherd's and Henriette Raphael Houses was opened. In 1994 the World War I memorial arch was moved and re-erected at its south end. In 2007 one of the Portland stone alcoves, originally from old London Bridge, was populated by a statue of poet John Keats by sculptor Stuart Wiliamson. In a rather different style and function is the undulating steel basket weave cladding to the new plant room at the bottom of Guy's Tower.

Guy's has always had a long tradition of medical education but this function has expanded hugely in recent years. Teaching at Guy's is in three divisions: medicine, dentistry and nursing. Until 1825 Guy's and St Thomas' co-operated in their medical teaching functions and these were reunited in 1982 by the formation of the United Medical and Dental Schools (UMDS). In 1998 these teaching functions were merged with the medical teaching functions at King's College and separate medical and dental schools were created.

The GKT Medical School is the largest in the UK with a total student body of around 9,300 (3,100 in nursing and midwifery, 2,500 in medicine, 1,000 in dentistry and 2,700 in biomedical and health sciences) and a teaching staff of over 400.

The GKT Dental institute is based at Guy's and at King's College Hospital at Denmark Hill, Camberwell. The first systematic teaching of dentistry in the country took place at Guy's in a series of lectures given in 1799 by Joseph Fox. However it was not until a century later that a separate dental school was established. It was also at Guy's where major advances were made in material that could be used for dental fillings. Dental surgeons from Guy's volunteered for service during the Boer War, the first time that soldiers were treated for dental problems during combat. More recent advances pioneered at Guy's have been in the field of forensic dentistry and surgery to reconstruct damaged facial features.

Aside from national institutions, in 1927 the Surrey Dispensary moved from Great Dover Street to 32 Trinity Street. For much of the post-war period it was used as a refuge for alcoholics until it closed in the late 1960s. The premises were converted into a private house and, for a time, were lived in by the champion of Shakespearian theatre, Sam Wanamaker.

Courts

While the Borough's prisons are now a thing of the past, the link with the judicial system has not been lost. Recently Borough has become a centre for legal activity and in particular for trying serious criminal cases in Crown Courts. The ten courts in the Inner London Sessions building on Newington Causeway were supplemented by a brand new court building, Southwark Crown Court, between Battle Bridge Lane and Morgan's Lane. This was opened in 1983 and its fourteen courts deal with criminal cases. In addition there is the recently-built Blackfriars Crown Court on Pocock Street. In all there are more than two dozen criminal courts in the area.

Backing on to the detached part of St George's churchyard is Southwark Coroner's Court. This has been here since the early 1940s and was incorporated into the site of the municipal mortuary. It was the office of the south western, later the southern district coroner. The post was appointed to by the LCC then the GLC and most recently the London Borough of Southwark. The building was modernised in 1961 and again in the late 1990s. For 22 years from 1974 the coroner was Sir Montague Levine.

City Hall
In the mid 1990s the More London Bridge site languished in stalemate, but farther along the riverfront was one piece of positive movement. The eastern end of the site was chosen for the site of City Hall, the

City Hall, 2008.
Illustration: Alan J Robertson.

headquarters of the newly-formed Greater London Authority. This much-needed, elected, London-wide strategic body is the effective successor to the Greater London Council, though it has considerably fewer powers. The building was designed by Foster and Partners, and Arup were the consulting engineers. The building is a decapitated offset steel and glass globe leaning back from the river, rather like a jelly in mid wobble. Its unusual design allows for maximum thermal efficiency in both summer and winter and visually for a light spacious interior by day and views into the building from the outside by night. The GLA moved in in summer 2002.

TRANSPORT
London Bridge Station
In the 1970s the exterior of London Bridge Station was substantially rebuilt (though the more radical rearrangement required to integrate the two distinct station areas into one was avoided). At the same time the bus station was added to the front and a pedestrian walkway erected across Tooley Street. The whole scheme is not a success. The overall effect is gloomy and much of the fabric is now dated.

Jubilee Line extension
The crucial feature of the area's renaissance in the late 1990s was the building of the extension to the Jubilee tube line. The proposal for a new tube line in central and east London had been circulating since the 1970s but the line was not given approval until 1993. Its construction took longer and cost more than first planned, but the project excels by its ability to carry very large numbers of passengers and in the designs for the new stations. The senior Jubilee Line architect Roland Paoletti appointed a different architect to each station. London Bridge underground station was designed by the in-house team under his direction. Its building was a major feat of civil engineering as the new ticket hall, which serves the Jubilee and the Northern Lines and links into the national rail station, is directly underneath Borough High Street and its construction (and the hugely valuable archaeological work that preceded this) was achieved by supporting the road while construction took place in the huge void underneath.

The line provides a fast link between the West End and docklands and has been a major catalyst in stimulating housing, office and leisure developments.

Thameslink 2000

Not all suggestions for enhancements to the railway system have been so popular. The Thameslink 2000 is hugely controversial. Thameslink is the only national rail service to link north and south London via central London. As part of proposed improvements to its whole network, it proposes to add two new tracks between London Bridge and Blackfriars and so ease this major bottleneck. This will allow additional capacity through central London and make proposals for new Thameslink destinations throughout south-east England viable. The proposal is to add two lines to the south side of the viaduct over Borough Market. This will be at the expense of numerous listed and historic buildings, which would be demolished; it would permanently alter the Borough Market, and the huge increase in train noise would interfere with the work of the cathedral and the surrounding area.

A public enquiry held between and 2000 and 2002 rejected the plan, and a second one in 2005, considering modified proposals on how to deal with destruction to the cathedral and Borough Market area gave permission to the scheme. Its supporters praise the transport benefits to cross-London travellers and the planned complete rebuilding, which by any measure is much needed, of London Bridge Station. Funding of £3.55 billion was announced in 2007 and works are expected to take place 2008-2011.

CHAPTER 5

Looking forward and back

For much of the last thousand years Southwark has been somewhere that has served London rather than been part of it. The functions of hospitality and food distribution most clearly exemplify this. However, developments of the 1980s and 1990s have reversed this trend and the Borough (and Bankside) have become part of central London. This process was initiated by office developments of the 1970s and 1980s, and the Jubilee Line and tourist attractions of the following decade. The Borough's landmark building is yet to come, but (subject to funding) will do so in the spectacular fashion of a 1000' (306m) high, 66-storey tower of tapering glass. Proposals for a huge tower to replace the one at the station were first released by developer Irvine Sellar in November 2000. The original proposals received a mixed reception but a new and slightly lower design by Renzo Piano has gained critical and planning approval, although not without opposition from English Heritage, sensitive to buildings that corrupt protected views of St Paul's Cathedral.

The Shard, as it is known popularly (but Shard London Bridge formally) is due to be finished by 2011 and provide office space for 5,000 workers, housing, hotel and public and leisure facilities, including a viewing platform at its very summit. The scheme will also provide for new pedestrian links from London Bridge Station to Guy's Hospital.

In April 2006 approval was given for a smaller tower, again masterminded by Sellar and designed by Piano. Unsurprisingly this was called the Baby Shard in popular circles, affectionately the Gem by its architect, but formally it retains the name of the building it will replace, the unlovely 20-storey New London Bridge House just west of the station. This proposal includes a new, and much needed, bus station at ground level.

With the precedent set for high buildings the Borough might provide London with a series of striking and very high buildings balancing those in the City and Docklands, radically altering the character of the area once again.

On the other hand, any of the more ambitious redevelopment plans proposed in recent years could now be in doubt after the financial turmoil and uncertainty of late 2008.

Visibly then the Borough might become a peer to the City of London, but the Thames means it will always be apart from it and make a very different contribution to the London whole. Like the City, the Borough has never principally been a residential area, rather its functions have been focused around commerce and communications. However, many of its present residents are fiercely loyal to the area and sensitive to plans that will undermine their quality of life. Like the City, it has a long, constantly-changing and distinguished history; this constant and often rapid flux is one of the chief attractions of the area.

Unlike the City, the Borough has been host to many of the features all cities have but few wish to draw attention to: crime, prisons, poverty, industry and immigration. This urban alter ego is what gives the area its unique character and has led to its unjustified neglect at the hands of London's historians.

If one theme emerges it is that the needs of commerce and communication prevail over people or welfare bodies. A road was the settlement's original raison d'etre; the inns dominated the medieval economy; the new approach to London Bridge meant the demolition and rebuilding of a significant part of the high street; the railways displaced thousands of people and ancient institutions; wharves and warehouses caused similar displacement, notably to an ancient church, and it has been new rail lines, office accommodation and, more gratifyingly, a rediscovery of the area's heritage, that has been the catalyst for its recent regeneration. The Thameslink scheme keenly illustrates the difficult balance between economic force and historic preservation, but the sober lesson from the past is that infrastructure has won over heritage. However the Borough is nothing if not resilient: the existence of the cathedral, a building with a feline instinct for survival significantly against the odds of history is evidence enough of this, and so whatever future residents, administrations, governments or entrepreneurs might bring to the Borough ultimately it will be its distinguished history, at the heart of London, but one remove from it, that will remain its enduring quality.

Sources

Books

Barclay, I, Perry, E, *Report on and survey of housing conditions in the Metropolitan Borough of Southwark* (Westminster 1929).

Bayley, E, *Newcomen's education foundation, Newcomen's clothing charity and John Collet's foundation in the parish of St Saviour, Southwark* (London, 1913).

Boast, M, *The Story of the Borough* (Southwark, 1997).

Booth, C, *Life and labour of the people in London.Third series, religious influences. Volume 4, Inner South London* (London, 1902).

Carlin, M, *Medieval Southwark* (London, 1996).

Chesterton, C, *I lived in a slum*, (London, 1935).

Corke, S, *Charterhouse in Southwark* (Godalming, 2001).

Darlington, I, *Survey of London Volume XXV. St George's Fields. The parishes of St George the Martyr and St Mary, Newington* (London, 1955).

Drummond-Murray, J Thompson, P, *Settlement in Roman Southwark, Archaeological excavations for London Underground Limited Jubilee Line project* (London, 2002).

Graves, C, *The story of St Thomas's 1106 – 1947* (Southwark, 1947).

Green, B, *Social reform and social change in the borough of Southwark, 1880 – 1930* (London, 2001).

Horne, M, Bayman, B, *The Northern Line* (Harrow Weald, 1990).

Inwood, S, *City of Cities. The birth of modern London* (London, 2005).

Inwood, S, *A History of London* (London, 1998).

Jackson, A, *London's termini* (Newton Abbott, 1969).

Johnson, D, *Southwark and the City* (London, 1969).

London County Council, *The housing question in London. Being an account of the work done by the Metropolitan Board of Works and the London County Council between the years 1855 and 1900* (London 1900).

Marcan, P, *Visions of Southwark* (London, 1997).

Owen, D, *The Government of Victorian London 1855 – 1889* (London, 1982).

Reilly, L, *Southwark: An illustrated history* (Southwark 1998).

Reilly, L, Marshall, G, *The Story of Bankside. From the River Thames to St George's Circus* (Southwark, 2001).

Rendle, W, *Old Southwark and its people* (Southwark, 1878).

Sharp, M, *My childhood memories of Mermaid Court, Borough High Street* (1993).

Steele, J (Ed.), *Streets of London The Booth notebooks, south east* (Deptford, 1997).

Sheldon, H, 'Roman Southwark', in Haynes, I, Sheldon, H, Hannigan, L (Eds.) London under ground. *The archaeology of a city* (Oxford, 2000).

Southwark Council, *Archaeology in Southwark* (Southwark, published annually 1993 – 1999).

Survey of London Volume XXII. Bankside. The parishes of St Saviour and Christchurch, Southwark (London, 1950).

Thomas, R, *London's first railway* (London,1972).

Watson, B, *Old London bridge lost and found* (London, 2004).

Watson, B, Brigham, T, Dyson, T, *London Bridge, 2000 years of a river crossing* (London, 2001).

Weinreb, B, Hibbert, C (Ed.), *The London encyclopaedia* (London, 1993).

Williamson, E, *London Docklands* (London, 1998).

Webster, D, *An illustrated history of Borough Market* (Southwark, 2006).

Wohl, A (Ed.), Mearns, A, *The Bitter Cry of outcast London* and reprints from the Pall Mall Gazette (Leicester, 1970)

Periodical titles
London Archaeologist

SLAS [Southwark and Lambeth archaeological society] News

Guy's Gazette

London County Council Annual abstract of statistics

InSE1

Other sources
Press cuttings' files on numerous subjects held at Southwark Local History Library

Ordnance Survey and other maps held at Southwark Local History Library

Index

Abercrombie Plan 109
Administration 28-31, 43, 73-4
All Hallows,
   Copperfield Street 77, 20

Bankside Residents Forum 112
Blackman Street 15
Borough Café 122
Borough Compter 43, 76, 85
Borough Market 51-2, 92, 121-2
Borough, the, character 1
Borough, the, definition 1, 43
Britain at War Experience 124
Burghal Hidage 14
Burial grounds 8, 20, 40, 78, 104

Calvert's Buildings 22
Cathedral School 45, 111
Chapter House 78
Charities 45-6, 59
Charles Dickens School 72
Charterhouse in Southwark 59, 112
Christ the Resurrection church 113
City Hall 127
City of London 29-30, 4, 76
Costermongers 96
Cotton's Wharf 118
Council housing 68-70
Courts 126
Crime 85-86

Dewrance & Co 94, 115
Drainage 15
Duke Street 107

Ecclesiastical Commissioners 61, 64
Engineering 93-4

Films 124
Fires 34-5, 92

Flemish community 27
General Strike 92
Geoffrey Chaucer School 111
George Inn 22, 34
Great Dover Street 105
Great Liberty manor 30
Guildable manor 29-30
Guy's Hospital 47-8, 81, 125-6

H M S Belfast 123
Harper Road Mosque 113
Harper Street School 72
Harvard, John 38
Hay's Galleria 118
Hay's Wharf Co 51, 90-3, 115, 116, 117
Henry Wood Hall 120
Hill, Octavia 66
Holy Trinity church 63, 120
Hop and Malt Exchange 89
Hop trade 51, 87-9
Horsemonger Lane Gaol 84
Housing 59-70, 110

Immigration 26, 43, 56
Industry 116
Inns 16, 20-1, 34, 50-1, 95-6

John Harvard Library 112
Jubilee Line Extension 33, 123, 128

Kent Street 104
King's Bench Prison 25, 40
King's manor 30

Lant Street School 72
Levine, Sir Montague 126
Little Dorrit 84
Lock Hospital 50
London Bridge 7, 14, 26
London Bridge City 117-8

London Bridge Hospital 18
London Bridge Station 6, 8, 82, 89, 96, 100, 102, 116, 119, 128, 129
London County Council 74
London Docklands
    Development Corporation 117-8
London Dungeon 124
London Food Exchange 90
London School Board 72
Londoners' stone 8-9

Maidstone Buildings 90, 100
Manors 28-9, 76
Markets 28
    see also Borough Market
Marshalsea Prison 23, 40, 83-4, 111
Marshalsea Road 106
Maypole Alley 62
Maze Pond Baptist chapel 81
Maze, manor of 30
Metropolitan Board of Works 74
Mint, The,
    and Mint Street 31, 33, 67, 83
Model dwellings 65-8
Morality 86
More London Bridge 118-9

Newcomen School 46, 71, 111
North Southwark Community
    Development Group 110, 112
Office accommodation
    and office blocks 116, 120
Old Operating Theatre 124

Parks and open spaces 87
Parochial administration
    see vestries
Peabody Trust 66, 78
Pilgrim Fathers'
    Memorial church 38, 113
Pink's jam factory 93

Poor law 44-5, 58, 83
Population 25-8, 43, 55-7, 107, 110
Post offices 84
Priory of St Mary Overie 16-7
Prisons 22-3, 40-2
Public health 46, 70-2
Pubs 122
    see also inns
Railways 99-103, 128
Redcross Cottages 67
Redcross Way 57, 65, 67
Reformation 17-19, 30
Rendle, William 71
Resurrectionists 83
Road layout 8, 16, 104-6
Roman period 4-12
Roman roads 3-4
Roman temple 10

Shard 130
Shops 96, 123-4
Snowsfields 68, 78
Social conditions 57
Southwark Cathedral 78, 113, 124
Southwark Coroner's Court 126
Southwark Crown Court 126
Southwark Diocese 78
Southwark Fair 29, 52-3
Southwark Heritage Association 123
Southwark Local History Library 112
Southwark Police Station 85
Southwark Street 105
Southwark, name 14
St Alphege, Lancaster Street 77, 113
St George the
    Martyr church 19, 36, 78, 112
St Margaret's church 19, 31, 34
St Michael and All Angels,
    Lant Street 77, 113
St Olaf house 93
St Olave's church 19, 36, 78-9

St Saviour's and
  St Olave's Girls' School 19, 35, 77
St Saviour's church   46
St Saviour's Grammar School   73
St Saviour's parochial school   73
St Stephen, Manciple Street 76, 113
St Thomas' Church   78
St Thomas' Hospital   18, 48-9,
                   81-2, 101
Stone's End   15
Strikes   93-4
Suffolk Place   16, 31, 34
  see also Mint, The
Surrey County   44
Surrey County Gaol   2, 4, 83, 84
  see also Horsemonger Lane Gaol
Surrey Dispensary   22, 83, 126

Tabard Gardens Estate   70, 110
Tabard Inn   20
Tabard Street   106
  see also Kent Street
Thames, River   21, 90
Thameslink 2000   128
Tourism   123-4
Town Hall   31, 41, 76
Trade   51
Trams   104
Trinity Estate   62-4
Trinity House School   111

Underground   102-3, 109
  railways   128
  see also Jubilee
  Line Extension

Vestries   43, 74
Viking raids   13

Wanamaker, Sam   112, 126
War Memorial   75-76
Warehouses   51, 87, 91

Water supply   71
Wellington, Duke of,
  memorial clock tower   107
Willcox, W H & Co   95
Winchester Palace and
  Bishop of   15, 17
Women's employment   94
World War II   107-9